Welcome to the Professional World

Success Principles for Entering the Workforce

Fourth Edition

By Gary R. Martin

University of the Pacific

Bassim Hamadeh, CEO and Publisher
Michael Simpson, Vice President of Acquisitions
Jamie Giganti, Managing Editor
Miguel Macias, Graphic Designer
Jennifer Allen, Acquisitions Editor
Brian Fahey, Licensing Associate
Sean Adams, Project Editor/Interior Design

First published in the United States of America in 2015 by Cognella, Inc.

Cover image copyright © 2014 by Depositphotos / boggy22.

Printed in the United States of America

ISBN: 978-1-63189-946-1 (pbk)/ 978-1-63189-947-8 (br)

www.cognella.com   800-200-3908

Contents

PRINCIPLE #3
Increase Your Cultural Sensitivity   49

PRINCIPLE #6
Optimize Your Time Management   91

PRINCIPLE #7
Exercise Good Judgment with Romances   115

Appendix A
Basic IRS Taxation Definitions and Model   127

Appendix B
Dining Etiquette   133

Appendix C
Business-World Jargon and Expressions   137

Appendix D
Internships and Cooperative Education   163

References   169
Editorial Thanks   171
About the Author   173

Dedication

To my wife, Nancy, for all her love and support throughout this project. To my parents, William and JoAnne, for all they have taught and continue to teach me. To my sisters, Judy, Linda, and Karen, who affirm me no matter how wrong I am. And to my wonderful children, Eric, Katie, and Will, who inspire me.

Introduction

"He came in here thinking he was all high-and-mighty, just because he had a college degree. He treats the admins and laborers like second-class citizens. And have you noticed that he thinks he's too good to pick up the main phone when the receptionist steps out?"

These are just a few of the infinite number of examples of mistakes people make when first entering the workforce. Some people make the transition from school to work right out of high school. Others do it after a bachelor's degree. And still others do it after graduate school. Regardless of how old we are when we first begin working in a professional environment, we all go through a similar learning curve that can be greatly expedited by learning from our predecessors' mistakes. That's what *Welcome to the Professional World* is all about—revealing the most common tricks and mistakes that can help or hinder your transition to the professional world.

When I show this book to seasoned professionals, the response is nearly always the same. They smile, nod their head, and comment,

"Yea, I always thought about writing a book like this." Again, *everybody* goes through this learning process. By cheating and reading about it ahead of time, you are sparing yourself much embarrassment, and you are empowering yourself further to focus more on the *technical* learning curve that also accompanies any new job.

This book is based 90% on interviews with people new to the workforce, along with their supervisors. I recommend you read it *before* you enter the professional world. I also recommend you review it *again* after you have been in the workforce for a month—you will see that many sections take on completely new meaning with your newfound professional exchanges.

Welcome to the Professional World is a collection of notes, resources, and short essays. This book will coach you with success-oriented fundamentals. Although some readers may find some sections of this book too elementary, that material may be the most valuable for the sake of reinforcement. Professional athletes learn the fundamentals of their respective sports long before they are drafted. Yet, as they venture on to compete at a professional level, they rely on coaches and trainers to continually reinforce the fundamentals.

"Keep your eyes on the ball!"
"Bend your knees!"
"Focus!"

Before you write off any of the fundamental coaching suggestions in the text that follows, you must first be sure that you are exercising that fundamental principle.

SO WHAT'S NEW IN THE FOURTH EDITION?

Much of this material is timeless. But much changes. We have updated and enhanced most sections, with the following more noteworthy additions:

1. The basics on financial planning and benefits
2. Many more bulleted do's and don'ts on work performance
3. Email ethics and efficacy
4. Work—life balance
5. Much more on the place of romances in the workplace

Best wishes in the Professional World. It's a jungle out there. But a potentially rewarding one.

Principle

$$\boxed{1} \quad 2 \quad 3 \quad 4 \quad 5 \quad 6 \quad 7$$

Get Your Financial Matters in Order

Money is power. Or to put it more respectably, money is empow-erment. The greater your equity (i.e., total financial worth), the greater your abilities to do what you want to do, and not do what you don't want to do. Financial wealth is a relative term. The same person can appear relatively indigent standing next to one person, and filthy rich standing next to another. It varies by your culture. This section will give you some encouragement to work hard, to exercise restraint, and to delay gratification. But most importantly, this section will give you insights on how to be smart. Like time management, success hinges more on working smarter than on working harder.

BUDGETS

You have to start out every year with a budget. Even a simple layout of how you plan to control your spending will go a long ways toward increased financial empowerment. But the more thorough, the better. Then you have to live by it, reviewing periodically.

A good budget helps keep you from over-spending, providing a strategic plan for maximizing personal, prioritized goals. So why do so few people budget their personal finances? Few people are this lackadaisical with their business finances. Most people seem to neglect the responsibility for their personal finances out of simple laziness, or the feeling that it won't really make that much difference. It does.

This chapter will present some basic ideas on how to put together a working budget. Everybody has their own way. (Even large corporations vary.) What works for you is all that matters.

How to Write a Budget

The following is a fairly detailed plan for someone starting off at a relatively modest wage.

Sample Budget

INCOME	WEEKLY	MONTHLY	ANNUAL
Income			$40,000
Total Income			34,000
Expenses			
Housing/rent		550	6,600
Home repairs and improvements			
Garbage			
Utilities		150	1,800
Telephone		100	1,200
Groceries	80		4,160
Laundry	10		520

Clothes		100	1,200
Dental/medical costs		50	600
Auto/gas	30		1,560
Auto insurance			1,000
Auto maintenance			600
Auto registration			190
Auto parking and permits			100
Life insurance			
Health insurance		50	600
Taxes (After refund – See Appendix A)			5,200
Soc. Sec. and SDI (Included in taxes)			
Entertainment		100	1,200
Religious institutions and charities		100	1,200
Gifts (e.g., birthdays, weddings)			1,000
Misc.		200	2,400
Total Expenses			31,130
Excess (to savings account)			$2,870
(Total Income minus Total Expenses)			

Income   The first thing you need to do is figure out how much disposable income you anticipate over the year. For most people starting off, this means just looking at your first paycheck and multiplying by twelve. Go to the trouble of figuring out how much you should have taken out of your check for taxes, and request your employer withhold that amount.

Ardent financial planners have the least amount taken out possible before penalties would be assessed. This way you will get more money each month that you can be investing. But remember that if you have too little taken out, you will end up having to pay a penalty at the end of the year. Many people prefer to do the opposite, having much more money withheld than is necessary. They like to get the refunds at the end of the year, and they view it as a forced savings plan.

If your company offers a retirement matching program such as a 401K, be sure to have the maximum withheld for the company match.

Eventually you will have other sources of income that you can factor into your budget. But for now, just look at your paycheck with the above factored in.

<u>Costs</u>   The second part of the budget lists anticipated costs and your gut-wrenching decisions on where you want to allocate your funds. This list must be comprehensive but can vary in the level of detail. For example, you could have an entry entitled "Transportation" to cover such items as car payments, gas, and car insurance, or you could have separate entries for each component.

You of course *have* to live within your means. Your costs can't exceed your income. Beyond this, you *should* make sacrifices in your life style for the sake of building up your equity. This is called delaying gratification. In other words, you *could* enjoy spending all your money immediately. But you *should* delay some of that enjoyment until a later time in life when it will bring you even *more* enjoyment, such as increased financial stability.

You in fact need to be working toward significant savings levels. Your first goal is to have enough savings that you could continue to live for three months if you were to lose your job. Next you'll want to work toward six months. And if not immediately, then at least very soon, you will need to be setting aside a minimum of ten percent of your income toward retirement. The later you begin this, wow, you will really regret it.

Most people start off living hand to mouth, meaning that they are spending all their paycheck every month just to cover their most basic needs. Even small amounts that you can set aside in savings each month will help you to move away from this challenging living condition.

A budget is a reflection of your priorities. If you have to choose between a membership in a health club, going to a few movies, keeping your wardrobe looking sharp and professional, a glass of wine every night, funds for family birthday and holiday gifts, personal vacation, … which are you going to choose? (Tips: There is nothing more important than your health. You MUST look sharp and professional at work. And I hope your family means the world to you.)

Realize that you will have surprises in your costs. Your car will suddenly need something major done. There will be an emergency in your family requiring you to miss a week of work. Some people create an emergency fund. I recommend you just recognize emergencies as one purpose of your longer-term savings plan.

A popular concept is that you should pay yourself first each month. In other words, there needs to be at least a little bit of funding allocated in your budget for you to have some fun each month.

Budgeting can be very complex. The tighter your funds are, the more helpful to have a more detailed budget. When I first started working, I enjoyed the above plan that includes weekly, monthly, and annual costs. It just allows you to look at the big picture more easily. Do your budget in an Excel file. It's easier and more fun to move things around and see the effects since many figures in a budget are derived from other figures entered elsewhere. (e.g., the annual housing expense is the multiplication of the monthly rent.)

COMPENSATION AND BENEFITS PACKAGES

Employers will have various ways they can compensate you, including myriad accompanying types of possible benefits. The following terms help to explain some of these.

Salary vs. Hourly (Exempt vs. Nonexempt): The Fair Labor and Standards Act (FLSA) requires that certain kinds of jobs be paid by the hour, but allows for other kinds of jobs to be paid by a monthly flat amount, regardless of how many hours the person works. Most jobs that are considered to be more manual in nature must be compensated by the hour, such as clerical and custodial positions. But many higher-paying positions also qualify for the hourly mandate. Some higher-paying jobs, however, like many management positions, tend to see the person work more hours some weeks, and fewer in others. These people are viewed more as extensions of the owners of the company. These people are often paid a salary, the flat monthly payment. So whether they work ten hours or fifty, they get the same pay. There may be lower levels of hourly accountability for these people. They may come in at flexible hours. Most of them probably end up working much more than the traditional forty-hour work week.

So the people who have salaried positions are considered exempt from the FLSA. They are called exempt employees. Their positions are called exempt positions. The people with positions who MUST be paid for every hour they work are considered to have nonexempt positions.

Benefits: The employer may also provide employees with the following benefits.

- **Retirement**—Some employers assist their employees with retirement savings. Normally they divert some money from their paychecks into a retirement account, usually contributing some additional funding themselves. They will often, match some or all of what the employee agrees to divert into this fund. The larger the company, the more leverage they may have in striking up more favorable terms with the company managing the retirement fund.

There are two types of these funds:

- **Defined giving plans**—These accounts are normally known as a 401K plan. All the money that goes into the plan, along with any appreciation over the years, belongs permanently to the employee. The employee is able to draw from these funds upon retirement.
- **Defined benefits plans, also known as pensions**—These work like 401K plans, except that when the employees retire, they are guaranteed a certain payout for the rest of their lives. So if you live a long time, you might have gotten much more out of the plan than if you had participated in a 401K. And if you do *not* live very long, then the plan emerges the winner.

  In both of these plans, the monies diverted from the employee's paychecks are tax deferred, meaning that they are subtracted from the employee's taxable income. But the employee will have to report *all* those monies when they draw them during their retirement, paying taxes on them at that time.

Other retirement savings vehicles that people often utilize in place of or in addition to the above company-sponsored plans include:

- **Traditional IRA**—IRA is short for Individual Retirement Account. IRAs are savings vehicles that people can use outside of company retirement plans. You can put money into these accounts for your retirement years. The money you put in gets subtracted from your taxable income, so that you pay less in taxes that year. You then report those monies along with any interest that has accrued at the time they are withdrawn. So the monies are considered tax deferred, which most people consider advantageous in the presumption that when they are withdrawn, you will be in a lower tax bracket, since you will be retired and not earning a monthly paycheck.
- **Roth IRAs** are similar to traditional IRAs except that:
  - The money put in is not tax deferred.

- The money and its interest or appreciation are not taxable at the time it is withdrawn.

- **Health insurance**—This can be extremely valuable since it is expensive to purchase on your own. Everybody needs to have it. Larger companies can negotiate lower rates with insurance companies, passing along these rates to their employees, along with paying a portion of the rate for you. It may also cover your spouse and children. Depending on the program you are enrolled in, you will likely need to pay a portion of the monthly premium, along with a co-payment each time you see a doctor, or receive any kind of service, or get a prescription. So for example, if you go see the doctor, you might have to pay $35 for each visit; and then your insurance covers the rest.

  You may have a choice of health care coverage plans, including:

  ◦ **Fee-for-Service**—In these programs you get reimbursed for much of your cost. You may need to pay a certain amount before you are eligible for the reimbursements. This is called a deductible. And you may be limited to a certain amount over the course of a year.

  ◦ **HMO**—Health Maintenance Organization. This is a specified collection of doctors and hospitals that you are limited to. These plans are usually less expensive, but perhaps less flexible, such as regarding which doctors you are allowed to see when.

  ◦ **PPOs**—Preferred Provider Organizations. In these programs you are given a list of doctors and other service providers. If you use these people, then you get reimbursed for your costs more than if you use providers who not on the list.

- **Dental**—This works the same as health insurance. But dental insurance and costs tend to be much lower.

- **Stock options**—Companies who are publicly traded can offer employees a specified number of stocks in the company for a given day's value, but the employee has six months after that date to decide if they want to buy them. So if the stocks have gone up in value during those six months, then they get to buy them at a bargain. But if they stay the same or go down, then they do not have to go through with the purchase.

- **Bonuses**—Some employers give their employees extra compensation at certain times, based perhaps on how well they do, or on how well the employer has done.
- **Relocation**—Some employers will reimburse new employees for some or all of their costs involved with relocating to the city where the employer is.
- **Company car**—Some employees are given a company car, normally as an allowance to support the employee for business-related travel. Check with your accountant on possible tax consequences with this.
- **Cell phone**—Some employers provide a personal cell phone to some employees, presumably to offset business-related phone calls.
- **Wellness benefits**—Some employers provide gym memberships to employees.
- **Continuing education**—Some companies pay tuition and/or other educational costs for employees, especially when it is related to their work.
- **Perks** (short for perquisites): A perk is some benefit that tends to be random, such as the company offering employees company tickets to professional sporting events or treating them to extra nice business meals.
- **Disability Insurance**—If you get sick or injured and are unable to work for a period of time, disability insurance will pay you a percentage of your normal income during this time. There are different types of these programs, varying in length of coverage, costs, etc.
- **Life Insurance**—If you die, your specified survivors will receive some predetermined amount of money. This is a way of providing some insurance and independence to your spouse and/or children. Many people do not purchase this, especially if they do not have a spouse, child, or other relative who depends on them. Often companies will help to cover the costs of it for you.

Some employers do not begin awarding you specified benefits until a certain amount of time on the job has elapsed (e.g., six months). Once this time has passed, your benefits are considered to be vested.

You should check with a Certified Public Accountant on all of the above financial matters for how they work with your particular situation. Many limitations, restrictions, and tax consequences exist, often varying with individual circumstances.

DEDUCTIONS FROM YOUR PAYCHECK

Your paycheck will have much money deducted from it. So if your salary comes out to $2,000/month, your check will be much less than this. Potential deductions include:

- **Federal withholdings**—You will need to pay federal income tax at the end of the year. But you are not allowed to pay it all at once at the end of the year. So most employers take some money out of each of your paychecks that they advance to the Internal Revenue Service (IRS). Then at the end of the year, after you file your income tax returns (one federal, and one for residents of all but a few states), you may need to pay more, or you may have had too much taken out and you will get a refund. (The best money managers do not have any more money taken out of their paychecks than is absolutely necessary, so that they can be investing it all rather than having it just sitting in the federal government coffers.) Your employer will have you fill out a W-4 Form. You will enter a number of allowances on this form that reflects how much money you think you need to have deducted. People new to the workforce usually enter one allowance. You could enter zero, but will probably have more taken out than is necessary. And you could enter two or higher, but will probably not have enough taken out.
- **State withholdings**—Same as the federal withholdings, except for the state. This is for people living in a state that collects income tax.
- **FICA** (Federal Insurance Contributions Act)—This is money that is matched by your employer to the federal government. Then when you retire, after a certain age, you will be eligible to receive a monthly

income called Social Security. You will also be eligible for free health insurance from a program called Medicare.

- **Health insurance**—If your company offers health, dental, and/or other types of insurance, they are likely requiring you to pay for a percentage of it. That will be deducted from your check as well.
- **Other**—There could be other expenses deducted from your paycheck, such as your retirement program, parking, and a health club membership. Your employer should explain all of these programs and options to you.

So when you get your first paycheck, you should go through each deduction and make sure that it makes sense to you. It is always possible that your account was set up incorrectly. It is up to you to check it.

TAXATION

Income taxation, in its most basic form, is a simple process that surprisingly few people understand. Like personal budgets, the level of complexity tends to increase with the level of income. As complexity increases, so does the likelihood that the taxpayer will need outside assistance (i.e., from a CPA). This section will briefly explain the principles behind taxation.

Gross Income:	Total income (from all sources).
Tax Deductions:	The government has specified certain types of expenditures as legitimate tax deductions or write-offs. These expenses can be used to reduce your taxable income. Possible examples are business expenses, charitable contributions, interest payments toward a home loan, and property tax.

Taxable Income: Total Gross Income minus all tax deductions and personal exemptions (one for each person in your household). Your tax rate is based on your taxable income.

TAXATION EXAMPLE

Suppose that you earned $28,000.00 in a given year. Suppose further that you had the following tax-deductible expenses and exemptions:

Charitable Contribution	$1,000.00
Home Mortgage Interest	$5,000.00
Total Deductions	$6,000.00
Total Income	$28,000.00
Total Deductions	$6,000.00
Total Exemptions (1)	$3,200.00
Taxable Income	$18,800.00

Suppose the tax rate for $18,800 is 10%. Then the federal tax you would owe is 10% × $18,800 or $1,880.

Again, this is a highly simplified picture of how taxes are determined. For a slightly more detailed illustration of this example, see Appendix A.

Keep Great Records: If you have an expense or make a payment for something that you want to write off, you *must* have proof in case you get audited. I personally keep a running spreadsheet that includes the date, whether I paid with a check or credit card, the check number (if I paid with a check), and a few words describing the expense. If I paid cash, then I save the receipt in an envelope. If you don't do this, then I can guarantee you, Murphy's Law, you *will* get audited.

Fallacy of "Overtime all going to Uncle Sam": How many times have you heard people say that they don't want to work any overtime because all their extra pay goes to Uncle Sam? It is true that as you make more money, the latter earnings are taxed at a higher rate, but the increase in the end is not nearly as high as some people perceive.

Fallacy of "Needing a write-off": To find a write-off, such as taking out a home loan, is beneficial only if you really valued the purchase itself. The fact that the expense is deductible does not increase your assets to a point higher than before you made this purchase. Ultimately it reduces the expense. For example, if you gave $1,000 to a charity, you might save $300 from your tax bill, but that still leaves you short the other $700. (But still give to charities!)

HOUSING AND RELOCATION

Employment opportunities often mean relocating to a new community. For help in the housing search, check the following sources for leads:

1. Online
2. Newspapers from the area
3. Employer in-house listings for roommates or rentals; ask the human resources office at your future employer if they publish a list of employees who are willing to rent a room; many employees have an extra room that they are willing to rent very inexpensively
4. College housing websites and bulletin boards in the area

CONCLUSION

Financial problems arise from:

1. A lack of financial planning.
2. A lack of resistance to sales pitches now that you have a regular and, in some cases, substantial income. Watch your impulse-buying habits since unbudgeted purchases, whether a few big-ticket items or many small ones, can quickly put you into a financial bind.
3. The illusions that somehow your financial problems will disappear or work out if you just ignore them.

In my countless interviews over the years with seasoned professionals, the three most common comments that they have given me are

*   I wish I had begun saving immediately.
*   I wish I had started a 401K (or IRA) when I was first hired.
*   I wish I would have planned for emergencies and set-backs by putting some extra money aside from every single paycheck, starting with the very first one.

Here are some final important suggestions and reminders:

1. Make a detailed and thorough budget and stick to it. If you go over in one area, adjust your budget to reflect the changes.
2. Set goals. When performance is measured, performance improves.
3. Build up a savings account equal to six months of your regular salary. This will bring you peace of mind and increased self-confidence, helping you to enjoy your work even more.

4. Own only one credit card, and set it up so that it is automatically paid off each month.
5. Do not rely on overtime to make more money.
6. If you are married, work and work and work at getting buy-in from him or her on the above.

Did I mention savings?

Put some money away every month.

A minimum of $100.

Maybe put it in a savings account.

Maybe in a mutual fund.

Then don't touch it.

Just leave it alone.

Forget about it.

Good luck with your finances.

Principle

1   2   3   4   5   6   7

Work Hard and Smart

Most people start their new jobs with only a rough idea of what they will actually be doing. In fact, most people don't even know exactly how they are going to learn how to do their new job. Thus, they feel a natural anxiety over their first day at work. Fear not. Just go to work ready to do your best. Your employer has committed to a major investment just by hiring you. They probably have a very good idea of what you do (and do not) already know. They will help you to climb that learning curve.

This chapter will coach you in some success-oriented fundamentals. This material will take on much greater relevance once you are actually immersed in your first professional work setting. If you are reading this *before* you have stepped foot into the professional world, then consider reviewing it a second time a few weeks after you have begun your first professional job.

APPEARANCE

1. Image is everything.

Pay attention to how your peers and clients perceive you. Many of the following suggestions refer again and again to this critical rule. People tend to remember negative perceptions about you more easily than they do positive ones. Make it a point to carry on all social conversations, personal telephone calls, and personal work during breaks behind your closed door or out of the office environment altogether. Conversely, allow your dedication and extra efforts to be visible, but with tact and subtlety.

> **Some exceptions?**—Be aware that in some company office environments, your boss or colleagues might not view your extra commitment and energies as a positive thing. Working extra hours after everyone has left for the day or taking an extra hour of work home might threaten them. Use your best judgment. Start by asking your boss.

2. Don't be TOO intense.

You don't want to come across as *overly* serious and tense. You may need to loosen up a little bit.

3. Pay attention to your aggressiveness and your assertiveness levels.

Work hard, and do not be afraid of trying new tasks that are within the guidelines and the purview of your job description. However, be careful and remember that when you speak your mind, you'll still be considered the new kid on the block for a while.

On the other hand, new employees usually enjoy a honeymoon period in new positions; they are given greater slack during their first months. Dr. Stanley Patterson, the past Chief of Cooperative Education Programs for the U.S. Department of Education in Washington D.C., once noted that the difference between an internship and that of a long-term employee is the

... increased tolerance or relaxation on the employers' part towards students' mistakes. This, of course, cannot be abused or taken for granted. However, students and new employees can capitalize on this a bit by opening up and becoming a little more aggressive in their assignments. (1988)

This would generalize somewhat to the new employee's honeymoon period as well. Seek a conservative balance between passiveness and aggressiveness.

4. Conserve your energy during the first few weeks on your new job.

The stress and tension of the first few days or weeks on your new job will be substantial. Reduce other activities and responsibilities outside your work as much as possible, and then slowly let them back in.

5. Use good judgment in taking too long at lunch and taking too many breaks.

Avoid extending your breaks to talk or just relax. You want to look like a team player and a hard worker. Many now subscribe to the motto that "Lunch is for wimps." Also, make sure you arrive on time (preferably early) and don't leave too early to go home.

6. Different organizations have different personal appearance and grooming standards.

You are constantly judged by your appearance. Appearance is the biggest factor in first impressions. You often don't know when you are suddenly going to meet someone who is important to make a great first impression on. And remember that you never get a second chance to make a good first impression.

But really, you need to make constant good impressions on everybody, all day long, every day. You need to look as attractive and professional and respectable and sharp as possible every single day. This includes grooming, attire, and physical fitness. Smiles help a lot too!

Our culture evolves in the area of attire. Many white-collar companies have moved toward business casual, a term that was coined in the late 80s (*Time* magazine 2008). But its implications continue to change, and vary by the specific company and type of work. Many find jeans and exposed underwear to be okay, according to 2008 surveys by Monster.com and Shopzilla.com. Other companies are becoming *more* conservative (*Time* 2008).

Before you begin your job, find out what the dress code is for the company's employees. If the code is more formal, this may be less comfortable to you, although in time you may become *very* comfortable with it. Other companies such as high-tech firms are known for more casual attire. Software developers, removed from scrutinizing clients, dress for comfort and creativity. Some people say that you should dress for the position that you aspire to. Most businesses insist that common sense and more-conservative dress prevail on days you face the public or meet the CEO.

Your appearance can help you get promoted or fired. Consider the following guidelines (*Development* 2000):

Women's do's

Dresses
Slacks, casual jeans
Blouses
Dress sandals
Blazers
Skirts
Sweaters

Men's do's

Khakis style trousers
Button-down shirts
Polo-style shirt
Sweaters
Jackets

Don'ts

Very short dresses and skirts
View of skin above pants
See-through clothing
Low-cut upper clothing
Tank tops or spaghetti straps

Don'ts

Sleeveless shirts
Gym wear
T-shirts
Ripped clothing

Don'ts for both

Worn-out clothes
Flip-flops
Shorts of any kind
Shirts with inappropriate wording/graphics
Anything too tight

Buy your professional wardrobe at nice clothing stores that have professional salespeople. They can help you make sure your clothes fit properly and that you are wearing them appropriately. Show them the combinations of what you plan to wear: shoes, pants, shirts, ties, dresses, accessories, etc. A few common pointers:

- Make sure your pants are not high-waters. They should at least go halfway down the backs of your shoes.
- Men's ties should go down to the middle of their belt buckle.
- Your jacket sleeves should go down to the end of your wrist.

7. Exercise excellent etiquette.

I recently had lunch with a junior-level manager from a reputable company who, after we had finished eating our meal, proceeded to lick each of his fingers on his right hand. Even little things like holding your fork wrong can mar your image. (See Appendix B, "Some Do's and Don'ts of Dining," for additional information on etiquette.)

8. Be yourself ... but be your very best self.

Make your best effort to create good impressions, but be natural and real and genuine about it. It's obvious when people are disingenuous. It works against you.

9. Look with your eyes and listen with your ears.

In face-to-face conversations, you'll make a much better impression on people if you form the good habit of listening before speaking. You can learn more and make a much better impression by being a good listener than from being a great talker.

10. Keep your office neat, clean, and orderly.

Your office directly reflects upon you. If it's always a mess and unorganized, that's how your peers and your superiors will think of you. Also be careful with food and drink around your desk. Orderliness will also increase your productivity and efficiency.

11. Avoid profanity.

It's a huge risk that isn't worth taking. Take the high road.

12. Uphold confidences.

The trite-but-true "Loose lips sink ships" is invaluable. Let the content of your conversation always ring with professionalism and kindness. The tight-lipped colleague who can maintain trustworthiness is exceptional. It can be fun and exciting to be the first to report dirt on people, but this talk comes back to hurt you later on.

13. Avoid criticizing the company, managers, executives, or fellow employees.

People sometimes are amused by these comments, but they ultimately hurt your image.

14. Be slow to offer constructive feedback.

Sometimes the new person in an organization will notice the company's quirks and problems early on. Suspend value judgments until you understand how and why the organization's corporate culture operates as it does. Frequent calls from a new employee to a supervisor to discuss how to reform or restructure the company may lead to the person being labeled a malcontent or upstart.

RESPONSIBILITY

1. Use a personal calendar.

Use an electronic calendar. You *must* have some kind of a written system for planning and scheduling events and responsibilities for any given day, including something that is to occur in three years. This is the first order of business in the category of being responsible. You cannot rely on your memory for appointments and other miscellaneous responsibilities.

2. Prepare a solid transportation plan.

It is your responsibility to be at work on time. Depending on the culture of your particular company, you likely should be arriving at least a few minutes early every day.

Your reputation suffers in the eyes of **everybody** who sees you report late to work, especially during your first few weeks on the job. No matter how late you work or how hard you work, you cannot make up for arriving late in the eyes of your supervisors, fellow workers, or clients.

If you depend on public transportation, be sure to check out the schedule carefully and give yourself plenty of time to make connections. If you are using your own car, then keep it serviced and in excellent working condition.

3. Review your employee handbook and other materials.

Many organizations publish handbooks and other materials for new employees. At least skim these. Unfortunately, many new employees never read them and wind up asking questions and wasting time when the answer was readily at hand. In general, learn everything you can about your company. It will help you start off on, and stay on, the right foot.

4. Daily logs.

Ask your supervisor if it is appropriate to maintain some kind of a daily log of your work. These can be extremely useful at times such as when you are working on annual reports. It also helps you to justify and account for your time with the people above you. (It's also interesting to skim occasionally.)

5. Keep family responsibilities to a minimum while at work.

It may reflect positively on you when family members pay you brief occasional visits at your worksite. Extended visits begin to work against you. If you have children, they should never be there killing time.

6. Avoid personal business on company time.

Employers have the legal right to check and monitor your computer and telephone, including email, voice mail, and Internet activity and content. New software continues to emerge that makes this easier for companies. A growing number of companies are reporting this practice. There is also software available that allows companies to track EXACTLY where you are through your cell phone if you are using a company cell phone. More and more companies are reporting this monitoring practice.

ADVANCEMENT

1. Seek to increase your level of responsibility.

This can be a tough challenge for many people, due partly to the fact that such advancement depends largely on one's supervisor. Many people feel additional frustration when they don't have ongoing assessment to let them know how they are performing and how they are being perceived. Just remember that this process is naturally slow and gradual. Some related tips:

    a. Do any and all work that you are given as well as you possibly can, and submit it on time. No matter how mundane or boring the task or project may be, or how many times you have done it before, keep up your level of professionalism and enthusiasm. (It is not uncommon for new employees to be given very low-level work initially. Be patient and positive; and know that your supervisor will be watching how well you handle this test.)

    b. Make friends with other professionals at your job site, especially the ones who appear to be well respected. Ask them for assistance and listen to their suggestions. Look over their shoulders, and offer to assist them, provided you have permission from your immediate supervisor. If your job has you too preoccupied during the day, offer to assist them by working a few extra hours at the office or at home. But make sure you do not sacrifice the quality or timeliness of your own responsibilities and projects.

c. Read manuals, annual reports, research reports, or anything else published by the company. Knowledge is power, and the more you know, the more you will be seen as an asset.

d. After a reasonable length of time on the job, let your supervisor know you would like to expand yourself professionally by taking on new projects and responsibilities.

e. After you have made overtures to your immediate supervisor for more responsibility, if nothing happens, be a bit more assertive and request more difficult and challenging tasks.

f. Volunteer for jobs and special committee assignments. You will learn more, and you will meet more people.

2. Ask questions, but learn to ask the right ones.

If you do not understand something, spend a reasonable amount of time trying to figure it out yourself. If you can't, then you should definitely not be afraid to ask someone for help or for a replay on a prior explanation. Learn to time your questions so you do not interrupt your supervisor or co-worker at inopportune times. "There are no stupid questions, only stupid answers." (Jerzy Neyman, Professor of Mathematics, University of California, Berkeley)

3. Put in some extra, un-clocked hours.

Manage your time well and try to work an extra three to five hours each week. Depending on your particular job and your personal level of ambition, many people are working fifty to fifty-five hours per week in order to get ahead. In addition to increased productivity and company competitiveness, this often leads to personal opportunities for new types of challenging tasks. (Note: I think most people exaggerate how many hours they work each week.)

4. Learn the company's computer systems and software.

This is a constant challenge that younger generations seem to conquer more readily than more seasoned staff. Students can often greatly enhance their individual value and carve out a niche for themselves by developing expertise with the company's computer systems and programs.

5. Seek exposure.

Get to know the people you work with on a personal level. It is equally important to help people involved with the company to get to know you. Such relationships can often be mutually beneficial. (More on this later.)

6. Take pride in your company.

Learn about your company's history and different projects that it has undertaken. This will help to make you feel more like part of the company.

The trouble with much of the advice business gets today about the need to be more vigorously creative is that its advocates often fail to distinguish between creativity and innovation. Creativity is thinking up new things. Innovation is doing new things … . A powerful new idea can kick around unused in a company for years, not because its merits are not recognized, but because nobody has assumed the responsibility for converting it from words into action. Ideas are useless unless used. The proof of their value is only in their implementation. Until then, they are in limbo. (1981)

7. Participate in company social events.

Opportunities like company seasonal parties and softball teams can help you to meet new people in the company, get to know others better, and build esprit de corps.

8. Persevere.

Younger employees often excel at work because of their upbeat and enthusiastic attitudes. Harvard's Theodore Levitt describes the benefits of perseverance in distinguishing innovation from creativity: **On asking for a raise ...** This is a tough one. There are lots of schools of thought here, including:

1. You should just trust your supervisor to look out for you and to treat you fairly. If you do a good job and increase your productivity over time, the employer will increase your compensation accordingly.
2. Greed is what the world revolves around. Your employer wants to make as much money as possible. So the more they give you, the less they are going to make. If you want a raise, you are going to have to demand it.
3. Just initiate friendly professional discussions periodically with your supervisor on the matter. Ask them how pay raises work, and then what kinds of things you need to be doing to warrant them. Keep it on their radar, but don't overdo it. Help them to appreciate that this is important to you, but put your main energies into doing an excellent job.

And just what are you worth? This is a good question that could probably be answered countless ways. What you happen to think may not matter if your employer doesn't agree. My favorite rule is simply that you are worth whatever anybody is willing to pay you. So if your current pay is $50,000 per year, and someone else is willing to pay you $60,000, then you have the leverage now to tell your current employer that they must pay this or lose you.

> **Gaining Cooperation from Others**
> - Talk to peers who enjoy a good relationship with the individual(s) in question.
> - Ask the right question. Be clear and direct. "I need your help."
> - Get your foot in the door: "Escalation of Commitment."
> - Find something to offer: "You've got to bring some to get some."
> - Acknowledge expertise or status: "You are the expert."
> (Source Unknown)

PERSONAL AND PERSONNEL

1. Make friends, but do not make close friends too soon.

There are too many little human relationship traps that you can easily fall into during your first days on a new job. One of these is building strong friendships too quickly. It is best during the first few weeks to concentrate on building modest relationships with all people rather than strong relationships with just a few people.

2. Respect everybody at all times.

Easier said than done. Remember, however, you never know who will be able to help you (or hurt you) a day, week, month, or years from now. Create allies, not adversaries.

3 Meet people.

Get to know as many people in the company as you can. Again, they may be able to help you some day. This is just as true for people outside your field of interest or in another department or division of your company. Here are some examples of department or division personnel you should attempt to get to know:

Technicians and specialists: Your work may bring you into contact with other technical specialists such as welders, electricians, and computer support people. These people can be of great help as well as a great source of grief to a young new professional. Seek to show respect for their work. Ask their advice and never try to show them you know as much as or more than they do about their work.

Human Resources (HR) personnel: The people in Human Resources can be a key source of help and information regarding personnel laws, benefits, company transfers, and other matters that your supervisor may not be aware of, or that you might not be comfortable discussing with him or her.

Administrative assistants (Admins): Your work (timesheets, travel vouchers, miscellaneous company forms, etc.) will undoubtedly bring you into contact with clerical staff. Do not treat these people in a subservient or condescending manner. Admins can make you or break you. Be cordial and respectful, and learn the office routine. As a new employee, the admin can give you important advice on office routines, various company personnel, and other crucial areas.

Company personnel: Find a company organization chart. Work toward learning names and faces of people with whom you come into contact and who form the top of the pyramid. The more you are able to recognize and greet them with respect, the more they'll be impressed with your knowledge and confidence. People like it when you know their name.

Clients: If your company deals with other firms, vendors, and/or clients, volunteer to run errands or deliver information or goods to these individuals or companies. Doing this can result in greater exposure for you with your company's business contacts. Making contacts or networking will always help you in moving up the corporate ladder.

Managers: Robert Half, a national authority on hiring policies, points out that managers usually prefer to fill open positions under them with people inside the company. These managers know that a lateral or a vertical move for an existing employee is a wise use of personnel and company resources. Also, promoting internally is a good way to ensure retention or longevity since these people already know something about the company. With this in mind, it makes sense for you to try to meet and get to know other managers. Among other benefits, these connections often lead to future job possibilities (1985, 32–34).

4. Avoid gossip.

Gossip can ruin the flow of production for weeks, and even years. Stay away from drama.

ATTITUDE

1. Don't flaunt your education and intellect.

Self-confidence and humbleness are not mutually exclusive—they in fact make for an awesome combination. Be approachable and teachable. Let your fellow workers gradually discover your educational background, skills, and abilities, only as it comes out naturally. Strive instead to build good relationships with those you are working with on a day-to-day basis. Let other people worry about recognizing you for your ideas and achievements.

2. Remember that you are young and new to the job.

As a student in school, you have interacted predominantly with other students who have the same general attitude about learning, social ethics and morals, and interests as you have. You have been surrounded by hundreds of people your own age. You may have been a big fish in your pond. This will completely change when you start playing on the company's turf. There are new rules, regulations, tactics, strategies, and skills you'll need to develop and learn. One of the biggest and easiest mistakes new professionals make when they get to their worksite is to have an over-confident or arrogant attitude. Recognize that you are young and suppress your big fish attitude. This will show some respect to people who are older and more experienced than you are.

3. Be a friendly and courteous person.

Signals of cordialness should be transmitted at every opportunity to acknowledge the presence of others and to recognize any courtesies they have extended to you, however small. The Carnegie Institute of Technology analyzed the records of 10,000 successful people and concluded that only 15% of what we recognize as a successful aptitude may be attributed to technical training, brains, and skills on the job. Around 85% of what we call success, however, is actually the direct result of personality factors such as the ability to get along and deal with people well. (Giblin, Confidence ...) Be fun to be around.

4. Take pride in everything you do, at work, at home, or in play.

Your work, like the office you work in and the desk you sit behind each day, also says a great deal about who you are and what your attitude is. Everything you submit to your boss or your peers should be as accurate, professional, neat, and clean as possible. Be careful, however, not to take this to an extreme by trying to be so perfect that you sacrifice productivity and efficiency.

5. Be positive.

Think positively. Act positively. Speak positively. People like to be around positive people.

6. Be willing to do ANYTHING! (that is legal and ethical)

Nothing should be beneath you. Similarly, pay attention to the duties of people around you so that you can fill in more easily if and when needed.

7. Acknowledge the work of others.

This will show self-confidence and build positive relations. People will like you more.

8. You are a developing professional.

In everything you do, think professionalism.
The following is a list of values I have collected and seek to live by:

Compassion	Can-do attitudes	Candor
Confidentiality	Diligence	Discretion
Enthusiasm	Equanimity	Expedience
Faithfulness	High energy	Honesty
Loyalty	Magnanimity	Passion
Positivism	Respectfulness	Sensitivity
Thoughtfulness	Trustworthiness	Upbeat
Unafraid of change	Unafraid of risk	Non-resistors
Change agents	Movers and shakers	Team players
Producers		

"The study of great accomplishments in art, industry, and science reveals a story of **the constant and purposeful application of talent and self toward a worthy end.**"

(May, 2007)

A POSITIVE ATTITUDE

(This section was guest-authored by the late Professor Thomas Cheney, former Assistant Dean at University of the Pacific.)

"Attitude" is a very commonplace and overworked word. You hear it almost every day. Parents talk about it. Teachers use it in class. Supervisors discuss it at work. No other word will have more impact on your future. Your positive attitude is your most priceless personal possession.

A healthy, positive attitude is essential to your success as an employee for many reasons:

1. You will be more energetic, highly motivated, productive, and alert.
2. First impressions on the job are very important because these impressions usually have a lasting effect. A positive attitude is the lasting impression you want to leave on your supervisor and fellow employees.
3. A positive employee contributes to the productivity of others. Attitudes are caught more than they are taught.
4. People on the job like other people who are interesting and involved with their work. These same people will shy away from other individuals who complain, contradict, or are generally negative.
5. The kind of attitude that management perceives will have a great deal to do with your future success.

It is important to realize that a positive attitude is far more than just a smile. Attitude is a highly personal thing. Then how do you make sure you keep your positive attitude when things start getting tough? Here are a few simple suggestions.

1. If you build a positive attitude in one environment or under one circumstance, it's probably more likely that you will be more positive and successful in another.
2. Talk about and dwell on positive things.
3. Try to always keep your self-talk positive. Self-talk is the conversation that is always going though your brain about what you do, how you feel, and how you are acting. The only time your self-talk headphone is off is when you're asleep.
4. Look for the good things in the people you work with, especially in your supervisors.
5. Look for the good things in your department, division, company and/or organization.
6. Don't permit a fellow worker who has a negative attitude to trap you into his or her way of thinking.

As the saying goes, "YOUR ATTITUDE SPEAKS SO LOUDLY THAT I CAN'T HEAR WHAT YOU ARE SAYING!"

THREE COMMON HUMAN RELATIONS MISTAKES
(By Professor Thomas Cheney)

ONE: Failure to Listen. Many excellent books and articles have been written about the art of listening. Most people need to learn how to listen and this means they must learn how to concentrate. Good, clear, and accurate communication is never easy. Sometimes it's very difficult just to sit back and listen. There are three basic reasons we fail at listening:

First: We are often so busy with our own thoughts and desires, related or non-related, that we are actually 90% a sender and only 10% a receiver. When this happens, the communications system breaks down.

Second: Some individuals are just too self-centered. Instead of hearing what is being said, they are always waiting for the other speaker to finish so they can then talk. So, constantly organizing your thoughts, and always preparing an answer for whatever the other person is saying at that moment will prevent you from becoming an effective listener.

Third: Some people spend so much time analyzing other people's motives or what they don't like about the other speaker's personality traits that they fail to hear what's being said. Here are some clues you may not be listening well:

1. Does the person speaking to you have to struggle to get your attention?
2. Do you find yourself thinking about something else the moment another person is speaking to you?
3. Does the person you are supposedly listening to voluntarily repeat his or her message? Or do you find that you regularly have to ask the other person to repeat a question or a statement because you missed it?
4. Do you sometimes feel confused about instructions given to you?

Being a good listener is not easy. It takes a real conscientious effort on your part. The following ideas should help you to improve your listening and communications skills.

a. Always look at the person who is talking to you. This will help you to concentrate and close out unimportant or distracting noises or thoughts.
b. If the person talking is having trouble speaking, you should be the one to make an extra effort to listen more carefully.
c. To help yourself remember the message or the instructions, take a notebook with you and write it down. Repeat it in your mind a few times. Then, when it's appropriate, repeat the message to make sure you got it right.

    d. Don't make excuses when people offer constructive criticism. You'll be surprised what you can learn when someone is sincerely trying to correct you or help you keep from doing something wrong.

    e. Think, reply briefly if necessary, and then continue to listen so that you'll receive the complete concept, idea, or directions.

    f. Always ask questions right away if you don't understand something.

    g. If you find yourself in a conversation with someone who is talking too much and completely monopolizing the conversation, don't hesitate to interrupt after a polite and reasonable period of time.

TWO: Failure to Understand Others. One of the biggest mistakes you can make, and perhaps the easiest one to make, is to underestimate the value and the potential contributions of other people in your organization. For example, many new employees take potshots at management. As a non-supervisor, new to the organization, you may not be in a position to see or understand the overall picture.

The smartest thing you can do is to avoid prejudging others. Be wise. Different people make different contributions to the growth, profit, and success of an organization. Top management can usually see this, but from your vantage point, you usually can't. Therefore, keep your impressions of others to yourself. Don't become a Monday morning quarterback broadcasting your signals and views all over the office. Remember, anything you say about someone may (and usually does) get back to them. There are few secrets kept in a company, regardless of the company's size.

THREE: Failure to Report or Admit Mistakes to Management. Everyone makes minor slips and blunders from time to time. Mistakes happen to the best of people, and unless you are an unusual person, they'll happen to you, probably when you'd least like them to happen. That's what Murphy's Laws are all about.

Most little mistakes, and sometimes even the big mistakes, are accepted and forgotten when they're openly and quickly reported to management. To try to cover them up is to ask for unnecessary trouble, which is usually more damaging than the original mistake. The best policy to follow is "If you mess up, fess up."

GENERAL COPING SUGGESTIONS

The balance of this chapter will provide specific suggestions from people in industry, some of them relatively new to the workforce, and others who have been there for many years.

We're Talking Basics ...

1. Do not call in sick when you are not sick.
2. If you are sick do not go to work. Otherwise you will hurt your professional image significantly. Even if you think you are no longer infectious, you should still exercise courtesy and sensitivity by not being in other people's presence.
3. Do not tell racist jokes ever, anywhere, including behind other people's backs.
4. Do not party too hard or stay up too late the night before work.
5. Do not load or play games on a company computer.
6. Always notify your supervisor beforehand if you are not able to come to work on a given day.
7. Do not take any property home that belongs to the company. Even a pencil or pad of paper. You should be able to afford to buy a pencil. Taking the littlest things home looks bad, and can lead to larger and larger things. This may seem obvious. Or it may seem benign. If it seems obvious, then I tell you that you would be surprised how often it occurs. If it seems harmless, then I tell you that many of your predecessors who thought

the same thing ended up missing out on promotions, and even losing their jobs. Just don't do it. The resulting stigma is horrible.

8. Get to know people's names.
9. Smile.
10. Be social, but limit social conversations to five minutes; your boss expects you to work, but understands the need to invest in some relationship-building.

Some Suggestions That May Be Less Obvious ...

1. Take the initiative to get the job done. This is the real bottom line. Easier said than done sometimes, but often if you just get started on SOMETHING, you will suddenly find it coming together.
2. At the end of your day, leave your area neat and picked up.
3. When you finish your assignments, immediately check with your supervisor for additional assignments. If nobody in the office has anything for you to do, check with other supervisors to see if they might have something for you to do.
4. Don't let yourself get stuck; try to solve problems on your own. But if you do get stuck for thirty minutes or more, ask for advice or help.
5. Keep learning more about new technologies.
6. Don't let leisure activities affect your job.
7. Take part in workplace activities and become a good team player.
8. Be conservative when using your company's resources.
9. Give sincere praise and credit to others for their contribution to a project.
10. Choose to think positively. When you choose to think positively, you become happier.

What I Wish I Had Done

These are the responses given by people in industry when asked the question, "What kinds of things did you not do that you wish you had done?"

1. I wish I would have taken more time to enjoy the job and what I was doing rather than putting pressure on myself to do better and work harder.
2. Kept my résumé up to date.
3. Continued to learn new stuff about my field.
4. Worked as if it were my own business, or as if I wanted to become the president. (Approach every job as if it will be a long-term position.)
5. Left my work at the office. This doesn't mean you can't take work home with you. It just means that you should have some down time to relax and do other things. It also means that you should not be depriving your spouse and family from getting a meaningful part of you each day as well.
6. Kept my education going. Above all else, do not interrupt your education to work for a while before you have at least completed your degree.
7. Taken a course in finance or accounting.

What I Wish I Had NOT Done

These are the responses given by people in industry when asked the question, "What kinds of things did you do that you later wished you had NOT done?"

1. Gossiped with co-workers.
2. Been so competitive.
3. Had a know-it-all attitude.
4. Not being outgoing or daring.
5. Not studying hard enough.

6. Headed for the door the minute my shift was over.
7. Worrying too much.
8. Hanging around other staff members who had poor work habits because I became associated with that style.
9. Too much partying and not enough time advancing my knowledge.
10. Listening to criticism and letting it eat away at me.
11. Complaining too much.
12. Getting too emotional about things.
13. Taking things personally that weren't about me.
14. Too much tunnel vision instead of exploring more in other departments and projects.
15. I did anything it took to make a sale, even if it compromised my morals and ethics.

Common Mistakes That People New to the Workforce Make

These are the responses given by people in industry when asked the question, "What are some common areas of mistakes you perceive that people new to the workforce commit?"

1. They don't take notes during the training period.
2. They don't get enough exercise or rest or both. They don't eat healthily enough.
3. They don't dress for success. Clothes really do make the person. People enjoy being around you because you look good.
4. They have trouble separating their personal lives from their professional lives.
5. Prideful attitudes. [If you are prepared to learn from anyone (regardless of background) you will go far. If you refuse to learn from others, you miss out on valuable lessons.]
6. They expect everything NOW.
7. Getting into debt.

8. They don't filter what they should and should not say when in a professional environment.
9. Making inappropriate (sexual) advances on co-workers.
10. Regularly attending to personal business on company time (online shopping, hours on the telephone, chronic absences during business hours, etc.).
11. They pretend to understand when they really don't.
12. Recognize that going out to lunch can be financially costly and time-consuming, and may be fattening. If you are also getting in quality time with key people, that can be good justification, but you should monitor this for all the above concerns.

Quotes from New Professionals and Their Supervisors

The following represents the responses made by past New Professionals and their supervisors when they were asked, "If you could make one suggestion to future New Professionals, perhaps based on a personal mistake, what would you say?"

From New Professionals

"Stress breeds stress; realize that a missed deadline or neglected priority is not a 'death penalty' offense. I often remind myself that the rotation of the Earth does not depend on my being involved in it. In other words, relax!"

"Study your previous course material."

"Be prepared to work a lot of hours."

"Be prepared to accept that you don't know anything."

"Keep an open mind."

"Don't worry about not having enough technical skills. Your work ethic and attitude are more important."

"Make contacts. Your first two to three weeks are often a little bit slow. Take advantage of this time and get to know other people around you."

"Learn when to stay out of the way. Project deadline day is not the time to try to impress your boss with your interest in the company. Pull back."

"In working with contractors, document everything! Conflicts seem to arise quickly."

"Develop a sense of humor. People who 'came up through the ranks' might resent a hotshot rookie and humor helps defuse situations. It also helps lighten things up when a superior fires orders at you and you do not have a clue as to what they are saying."

"Exercise communication skills. If you get conflicting directions from different supervisors, let them know."

"You're expected to know what you learned in school. Take key books from school with you."

"Do research. Learn new things. Investigate new things."

"Don't worry, be happy." Work is important but your health is essential.

"Demo brains; not legs." In other words, seek to impress people with your intellect, not your body.

"Don't take advantage of your situation. It's easy to shed responsibility by flashing a dumb look or developing the 'I'm just a rookie' mentality."

"Regardless of where you work or what you do, try hard."

"Live close to work. Two-hour bus and train trips one way are difficult."

"Don't assume you know what your superiors are telling you to do. If there is any doubt, ask them to explain."

"Keep on top of your work."

"Always think through a problem or idea thoroughly before presenting it to your boss, since her time is valuable, and you will seem more competent if you are always well informed. Be sensitive to all that is going on and learn the most from your experiences."

"I found I got along well with people by recognizing that my education was nothing compared to non-degreed colleagues who had lots of experience."

"Be open-minded and work hard to learn new things. It is absolutely possible that your career goals will change as you see what industry has to offer."

From Supervisors of New Professionals

"It is like the *Apollo 13* movie, based on the true account of when the space shuttle was trying to re-enter the Earth's atmosphere under emergency conditions. The commander enters the room and tells the engineers, 'Here is the problem. These are the materials available to you. And this is how much time you have. If you fail, the crew dies.'"

"Work for trust so that you will continue to get worthwhile projects."

"Never sit back and wait for 'work' to come to you. Always be proactive and ask 'What's next?' whenever you finish a task."

"It's good to be able to be a leader; at least a self-leader. You have to also be a good follower."

"Think."

"Take as proactive a role as possible in your new position. Volunteer, seek out different projects to work on, and make yourself known to your new co-workers."

"Have the mindset to 'get something done' that the employer can show as having value."

"Always carry a note pad, ready to take good notes of action items, instruction, times, and dates. This displays to everyone that you're not wasting their time asking questions that you will eventually forget. Many times simple instructions evolve into complex and detailed directions. If not written down, less than 80% of the detail will return with you to your desk. If you're writing instructions down, the boss is more confident the task <u>will</u> get done correctly. This may result in a steeper ramp of more responsible assignments."

"If you help everyone else do well, that will help you."

"Place emphasis on how you can best contribute to the organization you are working for, as opposed to what they can do for you. Individuals who want to change assignments for something they perceive to be more glamorous, or who spend all of their time trying to learn only what is interesting to them rather than what is expected of them, do not win as much respect."

"One of the first ways we evaluate our new people is by their initiative. When given an assignment and the initial instructions, the new employee is expected to find the related contacts and make the initial evaluation. It is easy to evaluate if the new employee has accomplished this by the next set of questions that they ask the person who gave them their assignment."

"If you aren't being challenged in your work, let your supervisor know. Don't keep it a secret. But don't expect to get out of other work that you find less exciting."

"Anticipate a burn-in period. It takes two to three weeks before a new employee can catch on to the system and start to become an active and productive member."

"Keep good records of your work and actions if a potentially unethical situation arises."

"Write legibly and with good grammar. Show calculations. Sign and date your work."

"It's not always best to try to get as much done as fast as you can. You must get it done well."

"Keep some balance. You will be more interesting if you have interests and commitments outside of work."

"When asking for time off, give four times the notice. For example, if you want a day off, ask at least four days in advance. If you want three weeks off, ask at least twelve weeks in advance."

"Always say good things about people, even if you have nothing good to say about them."

"Come early. Stay late. Work hard."

"Seize the opportunity."

Principle

1 2 **3** 4 5 6 7

Increase Your
Cultural Sensitivity

C onsider the following words and phrases, many of which can
provoke a variety of reactions, depending upon who is saying it,
and in front of whom:

Minority, minority affairs, diversity/diversification, inclusivity,
non-traditional populations, affirmative action, race relations,
ethnicity, people of color, underrepresented populations, multi-
cultural, African American, Black, White, Indian, American Indian,
Native American, Hispanic, Latino/a, Mexican American, Asian,
politically correct, ethnic sensitivity.

How open-minded are you? How fair are you? How do you view people
of different cultures, races, ages, genders, sexual orientations, and
physical abilities? When you meet people with different backgrounds

from your own, what do you assume about them? Are you interested in meeting them and learning of their interests, talents, and abilities?

New professionals entering the workforce will interface with people from a multitude of backgrounds. The businesses that are thriving are embracing this diversity in talent. This chapter will discuss basic cross-cultural ideas and assumptions, strengthening your sensitivities and cross-cultural skills in the professional workplace.

RELATED DEFINITIONS

In discussing this most sensitive topic, it is important to begin with some solid working definitions:

- **Culture**: The social heritage—the institutions, customs, conventions, values, beliefs, skills, arts, modes of living—of a group of people feeling themselves members of a closely bound community; and sharing a deep-rooted attachment and allegiance to that community. (Sue, 1981)
- **Stereotype**: A too-simple and therefore distorted image of a group, such as "People from the county of XYZ are always good in knitting." (Dictionary.com, 2007)
- **Prejudice**: An unfavorable opinion, judgment, or feeling formed beforehand or without knowledge, thought, or reason. (Dictionary.com, 2007)
- **Discrimination**: Any attitude or action that enables the subordination of a person or group because of color, gender, age, disability, race, creed, or national origin. (Sue, 1981)
- **Overt and Covert Discrimination**: Overt action refers to those actions that are easily visible and identifiable as discriminatory (e.g., throwing rocks, telling racial jokes, etc.). Covert discrimination is much more subtle in that it frequently involves the lack of action, or action that seeks justification on different grounds (e.g., lack of positive personal feedback, institutional policies that have negative consequences when race, sex, age, etc., is considered despite "well-intentioned" goals). (Sue, 1981)

COLORBLIND/CULTUREBLIND

"Colorblind" is a figurative term meaning that you view and treat others as if there were no difference between yourself and people of different races and ethnicities. Whether a person is colorblind is an interesting question. Many would suggest that nobody is truly colorblind in treating people from different racial, ethnic, or cultural backgrounds the same, and fairly. Do you speak in exactly the same way, and as freely, in front of people of all backgrounds? Do you tell the same stories? The same jokes? Make the same observations or recommendations? Would you marry a person of any color? Would you allow your daughter or son to? If you answered "no" to any of these questions, does that mean you are a racist?

Should we be colorblind? Up until the late 70s, the answer appeared to unanimously be "yes." Then the Platinum Rule emerged, challenging the Golden Rule. Whereas the Golden Rule suggests that we should treat people the way we want to be treated, the Platinum Rule suggests that we should, "Treat others as they would have us treat them." The assumption here is that people tend to vary culturally in various ways including how open they are, how confrontational they are, their typical personal space, and how they view family life.

Factors such as your race, where you grew up, your religious views, and your economic status tend to influence your personality, character, values system, as well as your cultural response to others. The Platinum Rule suggests that we learn to appreciate these differences in other people, and seek to respect the differences in others as we interact with them. Dr. Derald Wing Sue defines "color blind" as:

> The denial of another's culture (e.g., race, national origin, religion, sex) as an attribute which affects their behavior and personality. This philosophy, which may be more

appropriately termed "culture blind," promotes treating different people in "equal" ways despite the fact that individual histories may call for different solutions. A philosophy which promotes "equal treatment" (e.g., "I don't even think of someone as Black, White, Jewish, a woman, etc. I just think of them as people.") at the expense of "fair treatment," (i.e., respecting and accommodating individual cultural differences) contradicts the notion of cultural pluralism. (1981)

"Valuing differences" is a longstanding and important theme in corporate America, proffering the idea that a diverse pool of talent can be stronger as a team than a team composed of homogenous or mono-cultural individuals. Many Americans promoted for a long time the melting pot concept that suggested people of different backgrounds should all begin to assimilate into a homogenous American culture. The early 80s produced the alternative concept of the salad bowl, which suggests that salads are richer with a variety of distinct ingredients.

Consider some of the following examples of potential cultural differences between people:

CULTURE A	CULTURE B
Individual is the source of good ideas	Science is the source of good ideas
We should compete with each other	We should cooperate with each other
Families should respect the opinions of children	Family is a hierarchy and children must obey
Autonomy is encouraged	Subordination is encouraged
We are a team	We are a community
We prefer aggressiveness, kick-tail style	We practice the Golden Rule
The customer is always right	We know what's best for the customer

You will sometimes tend to agree with one side or the other of the above contrasts, varying with your particular cultural background. But more importantly, you will hopefully be able to see that both sides are understandable and that different does not necessarily mean worse.

Stephen H. Rhinesmith has done some similar research that he reports in his book *Bring Home the World*. He suggests that there are assumptions or values held by the majority of Americans, and that there are others held by the majority of persons of a Contrast American Society. Consider a few of his related observations:

HOW DO WE SEE OURSELVES?	AMERICAN	CONTRAST AMERICAN
What is our primary identification?	Within ourselves as individuals	As part of a family, clan, caste, or tribe
What do we value in people?	What people can achieve through special skills	A person's background, family connections, tribal affiliation
Whom do we rely on for help?	Ourselves as independently resourceful people	Our friends, family, and others owing us obligations
How do we learn about life?	From personal experience	From the wisdom and knowledge of others

HOW DO WE SEE OUR RELATIONSHIPS WITH OTHERS?	AMERICAN	CONTRAST AMERICAN
How do we relate to people of different status or authority?	Minimize the difference; take for granted everyone's the same	Stress the differences; show respect for authority/position
How do we idealize work and sex roles?	Little differentiation between male and female roles	Distinct and rigid differentiation between male and female
How do we idealize sex roles and friendship?	People may have close friends of both sexes	People may have close friends of same sex only
How do we deal with conflict?	Favor eye-to-eye confrontation between the two people disagreeing	Find it unacceptable and embarrassing
What is the preferred pace of life?	Fast, busy, conducive to getting things done	Slow, steady, conducive to getting the most from life
How do we regard kidding or joking at the expense of others?	As acceptable, interesting, and fun	As unacceptable and embarrassing

HOW DO WE SEE THE WORLD?	AMERICAN	CONTRAST AMERICAN
How do we look at time?	In precise minutes and hours by which we organize our days	In diffuse days, weeks, or months by which we organize our years
How do we measure progress?	In concrete, quantifiable units that indicate amount, size, percent and the like	Against abstract social and moral principles of our society

(Rhinesmith, 1975)

Again, your values will likely vary by your particular background. You can begin to feel a tension between a traditional American values system and values that might be held by others in your workplace and business contacts. As we discover cultural differences, we need to be sensitive to them, work with them, and ultimately, appreciate and value them. When people want to talk to you about their culture, listen and show interest. You will honor them by doing this, and you might learn something.

RACISM, SEXISM, AND OTHER ISM'S

Why do people treat other people of different backgrounds unfairly? What is this based on? In the case of racism, you might think that these biases are based on differences in physical characteristics. This is often untrue. For example, although conflicts between these groups have been intense, there is little or no difference in physical characteristics among Germans and Jews in Europe, Iraqis and Kurds in the Middle East, and Hutus and Tutsis in Rwanda.

The roots for sexism are more apparent, given observable physical differences between the sexes. Still, one would not think that educated and enlightened professionals of our era would continue to stereotype others based on their gender.

This chapter aims to help the reader understand the "what's" more than the "why's," so that you can interact and team productively and more harmoniously with people from backgrounds different from your own. Many have sought to make light of this goal, labeling culturally sensitive behavior as politically correct. My suggestion is that you err on the side of being *too* sensitive.

The following are some of the most common violations of cultural sensitivity:

- Do not refer to women as girls or gals, or to men as boys.
- Do not use the male pronoun as gender neutral. Instead, use "him or her" and "she or he." Or use plural pronouns (e.g., they and them), which are *always* gender neutral. Limit the use of male pronouns to specific male persons. For example, avoid referring to a doctor or engineer as "him," unless you know the person is in fact a male.
- Avoid expressions that use the word "black" pejoratively.
- Do not tell racial or gender jokes. If someone tells you a racist or sexist joke, remember that if you even smile in response, you are sending the message that you support such behaviors or attitudes.

Stereotypes in the Workplace

There are lingering myths and stereotypes in the workplace regarding different populations that are reprehensible for anybody to suggest or joke about. These can be based on gender, race, culture, age, religion, or other differences. The following is a small sampling of offensive stereotypes:

- Always late
- Have poor grammar
- Cold, rude, anti-social, and/or indifferent
- Dishonest
- Prone to alcoholism or illegal drugs
- More likely to be involved with crime
- Mentally slow
- Lower learning aptitude
- Insensitive

- Too sensitive
- Timid
- Talkative
- Untrustworthy

Get rid of any disparaging generalizations you have about specific cultures or populations. They are incorrect and harmful.

Sexual Harassment

Title VII of the Civil Rights Act of 1964 made sexual discrimination in the workplace illegal. The Equal Employment Opportunities Commission has since produced guidelines to define sexual harassment. The behavior must contain the following three elements:

1. *It must be sexual in nature.* Even a foul or vulgar joke, though inappropriate, might not be sexual harassment if it did not include some sexual aspect.
2. *It must be unwelcome.* Colleagues can have romantic relations with each other or share lewd jokes with each other, as long as these acts are consensual.
3. *There must be discrimination based on gender.* (Government code)

Harassment is often characterized by the undue exercise of power by a superior over a subordinate. Proposing sex in exchange for a raise is sexual harassment at its most blatant. But sexual harassment can take more subtle forms. Consider the following interview:

> **Employer (E):** Good afternoon Ms. Lopez, I'm Bill Johnson, H.R. Manager of St. Mary's Hospital. Thank you for coming in today. Did you have any trouble finding us?
>
> **Prospective Employee (P.E.):** Thank you Mr. Johnson. No, your directions were very clear.

E: Please call me Bill. We have a very friendly organization here, just like family. I want the girls who work here to think of me as their dad. Elizabeth, please tell me a little about yourself.

P.E.: I am a second-year student at Nelson's College of Radiology. I will complete my final coursework in January and will receive a degree and my license at that time.

E: We are looking for someone who is attractive, friendly, and can really sell our clinic to customers who call or come in. You certainly are pretty enough. What previous work experience have you had?

P.E.: I have worked as an X-ray technician intern at Sutter Hospital the past year. Before that, I worked a couple years as a counter person at Burger King.

E: As you can see, Liz, we are a very small office and I need someone who will be here every afternoon. You aren't going to get married and pregnant on me are you? The last gal we had I spent three months training and then she went and fell in love with one of our patients. I told her she was making a big mistake but she just wouldn't listen.

P.E.: No, Mr. Johnson, I am very dependable. My internship records will show that I have only missed two days of work this past year because I was ill. Overall my attendance has been very good. I understand the importance of having someone to cover the office and, if hired, you would have a very reliable employee.

E: What about transportation? Do you have a car or am I going to have to be picking you up down at the bus stop every day? I have done that for some of our other girls but I'd rather not.

P.E.: I do not have a car, Mr. Johnson, but I will take care of my transportation. I get up early and will have no problem being at work on time.

E: Well, if you need a ride, you can just call me. My biggest concern for this position is that the person we hire is friendly and nice to the clients. Sometimes it even helps if you flirt a little with the guys that come in. I know you can do that, can't you?

P.E.: I will be friendly with all the clients.

E: Well, honey, I think you will be just fine but we have a couple of other girls to interview. I'll be making my decision by the end of the week. I will let you know if you're the lucky lady.

P.E.: Thank you very much, Mr. Johnson, for your time and the interview.

Demeaning and unprofessional exchanges not unlike the above continue to occur in the workplace. Although it is usually a woman who is being victimized, men can also find themselves victims of unfair and derogatory treatment based on their gender.

Almost all sexual harassment falls into one of two categories: quid pro quo harassment and hostile work environment harassment. Quid pro quo is "Something for something": "You give me this, and I'll give you that in return," e.g., "Give me sex and I'll give you a better job." A hostile work environment is when a person is forced to work in a setting where there are excessive sexual jokes, gestures, etc. Avoid the following behaviors, which are or might be considered sexual harassment:

- **Inappropriate remarks**. For example, complimenting people's legs, saying you had a dream about them, etc.
- **Sexual generalizations and put-downs**. For example, saying men are too insensitive.
- **Terms of endearment**. For example, calling someone "Cutie."

- **Nicknames**. For example, referring to someone as "Hot Stuff."
- **Suggestive compliments**. For example, telling someone you like the way his or her clothing fits.
- **Wandering hands**. For example, back-rubbing, knee-touching, handling people's clothing or jewelry.
- **Corporate kissing**. (Stick to handshakes.)
- **Making eyes**. For example, prolonged staring or looking at a person below their face.
- **Taunting and teasing**. For example, heckling.

The following are a couple final examples of inappropriate sexually related conduct, each as reported by new professionals:

"The wage-workers and I joked around a lot. One day, I made a joke to one of the guys and then I said, 'No. I'm just teasing.' He responded, 'Oh, are you a tease?' I responded sternly, but with a slight smirk to keep from sounding overly serious, 'No I'm not and you're not supposed to talk to me like that.' We all remained on good terms and nobody ever tested me again."

"I accepted a position in which my supervisor and I had to conduct a lot of work together, including extensive travel alone, and staying overnight in hotels (in separate rooms). My supervisor seemed to develop feelings for me, but I did not reciprocate at all. Unfortunately, his feelings seemed to persist. He never really said or did anything that would sound that bad, but asking me things like how things were going with my boyfriend, or just touching my hand once in a while to get my attention made me extremely uncomfortable."

Sexual harassment is widely acknowledged as UNACCEPTABLE. Lawsuits abound. The great majority of cases are by women against men, but some are the reverse, and some are between people of the same sex. Assess your mindset with regard to the opposite gender from a professional standpoint. Abolish any attitudes that may be the least bit professionally unequal, unfair, disrespectful, etc. And as far as humor goes, "Don't go there." It's not funny. Even a small comment that seems completely harmless can get you into more trouble than could ever be worth it.

Discrimination

Illegal discrimination occurs when people are treated unfairly based on race, gender, etc. Fairness is important to all of us at all times. Many women and people of color perceive a glass ceiling in their places of employment. A glass ceiling is a figurative barrier that prevents people from advancement to higher levels. You can see the higher positions through the glass ceiling, but you can't seem to get there on your qualifications and merit.

When you perceive discrimination or reverse discrimination, your response can range from complete complacency to vigorous protests. You will have to decide for yourself the most prudent response, taking into account the possible risks, ramifications, and consequences. My strong suggestions are

1. Do not respond immediately. Wait at least one day.
2. Talk to at least two other people before taking any action.
3. If you do decide to respond, refrain from appearing to jump to conclusions. Give the person you believe may have discriminated against you the benefit of the doubt, and phrase your concern as a question. Ask them for the basis of their decision or action. Give them a chance to explain or clarify their behavior and intentions.
4. If you still feel that you have been discriminated against, then your next step is to document your grievance in writing. This documentation may be helpful when you are ready to discuss the incident with others. You should also find out what your company's protocol is and follow it. In some cases, your first point of contact is your supervisor. If your grievance is against your supervisor, then you should report your concerns to your supervisor's supervisor. If after that, you still don't feel that the situation has been handled appropriately, then the

usual next step is to speak with a representative in your human resources office. In addition, many companies have an impartial ombudsman who deals with complaints such as these. Whatever the case, follow protocol and document all aspects of the process.

CONCLUSION

We prosper when we move from viewing diversity as a problem to viewing it as an advantage. Margaret Visser writes that:

> *Machines like, demand, and produce uniformity. But nature loathes it: her strength lies in multiplicity and in differences. Sameness in biology means fewer possibilities and therefore weakness.* (1986)

Principle

1 2 3 $\boxed{4}$ 5 6 7

Exercise Discretion

S tudents get tired of hearing about the real world, as if school were a world that's make-believe. A collegian once expressed this sentiment in a school paper, stating that "... college is comparable to the 'real world' since rigorous work exists and results in its own payoffs." Nonetheless, most would agree that there are major differences between the work environment and the college campus, differences that need to be accommodated in making the transition from school to work, with less stress and more success.

DIFFERENCES BETWEEN SCHOOL AND WORK

The following are some differences between the academic and workplace environments.

Feedback: Instead of grades, feedback on a professional assignment can be both formal and informal. Examples are weekly meetings, daily statements, and annual evaluations. Some supervisors tell you only what you are doing wrong, not when you're doing something right. A good supervisor will track you only to the extent needed.

Accountability: Accountability issues are also different. In school, the work you do usually only affects *you*. You earn *your* grade—no one else's. However, as a professional, you are often a part of a team. In such situations, your efforts directly affect others, and vice versa. Even if you function independently as a professional, you're still part of a group (i.e., your department, research unit, division, etc.), and your performance impacts directly upon that group and the project's success.

There's no longer just one correct answer:

When you are in school there is often just one correct answer. In the business world, there's rarely just one answer. Instead, a good professional has to weigh all the alternatives and choose the best option given the goals, budget, and resources of the company at that given moment. Most of the time it means wearing many different hats: communicator, manager, public relations specialist, accountant, marketing manager, customer service representative, and others.

Partial credit: When you work on the above answer, there will not be any partial credit. You must persevere on a project until it is completed and working.

Time: Time concepts may be different. In school, students tend to mark the passage of time by semesters, quarters, or by the number of weeks until exams. In the working world, people think in terms of fiscal calendars, project schedules, duration of advertising campaigns, product life spans, and other time structures related to the work world. It seems as though there are fewer end points and more starting points to choose from (Student to Professional ... 1987).

Unlike life as a student, you can't get away with cramming the night before as a professional. Deadlines change. Progress reports are often required with almost no time to put them together for management. There are seemingly constant interruptions that work against you at every step along the way.

At school, many students routinely sneak into class ten minutes late. At work, people notice when you come and go, and judge you accordingly.

At work, you have project schedules and a calendar. Jobs are usually ongoing rather than sectioned. Also, at work you are confined to one place and time frame, unlike the off-and-on schedules at school (Student to Professional ... 1987).

Teamwork: At work, collaboration is not cheating. One new professional noted, "In school you write the computer code until it works. But in industry, the code must be structured so it's easily readable if others need to read it and modify it."

Chain of command: At work, you must also learn and respect the chain of command. This is HUGE in industry! It is completely non-existent in school.

Limited resources: What motivates managers is summed up in the old business phrase "Under budget and on time." All of a sudden, time and money must fit inside new constraints. At school you can often spend lots of time and limitless lab resources on projects.

Etiquette: Business, phone, email, and general etiquette may sometimes be underrated by new employees. Letitia Baldrige wrote *The Complete Guide to Executive Manners*, in which she notes that today, when business is done not only in the boardroom, but in planes, restaurants, the company car, at home, and in other countries, studying etiquette can help you to perform flawlessly, with poise and confidence, in every business-related situation. Etiquette is about the importance of detail and about how details linked together can create the strong, effective executive presence that propels an individual upward in his or her career (Baldrige 1985, Cover, 3).

Etiquette can be extremely helpful with such areas as:

- Guidelines for working with the opposite gender
- Entertaining business groups
- Writing emails
- Running successful meetings

To just give one example, I learned from such a book the idea of stepping out of a crowded elevator at each stop when I'm near the door, just to make it easier for people in the back to get out. Then of course I step back in after they have exited.

Consider finding a resource on etiquette and reviewing it once in a while. You'll learn a lot of great tricks that enhance your decorum.

Physical Appearance

You have to *be* good, and you have to *look* good. There is much overlap between these two goals, but certainly not 100%. On the Looks side, consider:

1. **Dress for success**. When you dress like a professional, you'll begin feeling, acting and talking like a professional. If you dress like a slob, you'll be telling everyone at work that you are a slob.
2. **Grooming is also crucial for success**. Grooming includes keeping your shirts, pants, dresses, and other garments washed and ironed, your shoes polished, your hair nice, and your body clean. Nothing is worse than being in a closed-session meeting, in a small conference room, with someone who doesn't bathe every day and who doesn't use deodorant. By the way, most people can't tell when their clothes smell from body odor. Most garments should be washed after one day's use. Brush your teeth and use mouthwash and or mints regularly.
3. **Every work site has a corporate culture that is more than just a dress code**. There is a style of doing business, how the

company views its employees, and what value the company places on security, dedication, and loyalty. It's up to you to learn as quickly as possible what the culture is like and either choose to adapt (because you feel comfortable with the culture) or decide that you cannot buy into the culture and leave. But while you are there, don't try to fight the company's culture. Do your best to fit in and honor it.

ETHICS

Many new professionals are surprised with the ethical issues they face on the job. They may become concerned with the product or service provided by the employer. They may question methods used by co-workers. They may feel uneasy about their own involvement in certain actions. These situations raise questions that are difficult but extremely important to face (Student to Professional ... 1987).

Plato's observation that "the unexamined life truly isn't worth living" emphasizes the importance of examining and understanding your personal values. These internalized standards should be your guide in any situation of potential ethical conflict. What is acceptable for someone else may not be acceptable for you (Ibid.).

The subject of ethics has been highly researched, debated, and published. It is offered as a course at most colleges and universities. Professional schools are usually required to address the subject at a minimum level for accreditation purposes. (Many professions such as law have their own specific codes of ethics.) For this reason, the subject of ethics is only briefly presented here. Responsible professionals will make ethics a subject of lifelong learning through professional journals, conferences, etc.

A Definition of Ethics

Some past philosophers have defined "ethics" as follows:

A Concern for Good Behavior. Ethics is the name we give to our concern for good behavior. We feel an obligation to consider not only our personal well-being, but also that of others and of human society as a whole.

A Study of Human Actions. Ethics is a systematic study of human actions from the point of view of their rightness or wrongness as a means of achieving ultimate happiness.

A Science of Right and Wrong. Ethics is the science that deals with conduct, insofar as this is considered as right and wrong, good or bad.

Code of Morals. Ethics is a system or code of morals of a particular person, religion, or group.

Science of Values. Ethics is a science of determining values in human conduct (*Engineering Education*).

The most popular rule of ethics is the Golden Rule (which shows that the subject of ethics dates back at least to the times of Jesus Christ, Confucius, and the Buddha). As simple as the Golden Rule may seem, its implementation is far from so. Consider just a few examples of popular ethical dilemmas:

- Capital punishment
- Abortion
- Euthanasia
- Eugenics
- Stem cell research

Ethics is not just a conversation piece for distinguishing moral standards among colleagues and friends. Ethical questions can carry serious financial and/or legal implications. Corporation executives go to prison and/or pay immense fines for such ethical violations as lying or even withholding the truth. An employee can be charged with a felony for lying, even if the employee was told to lie by an employer. This is referred to as the Good Soldier Complex. The Nazi German soldiers claimed that they just did what they were told to do. Yet many of them were held accountable after World War II came to an end (Wujek 1988).

Common Ethical Issues

Some common ethics issues list as follows:

1. Conflicts of interest
2. Plagiarism, copyright violations (printed, software, photos), aka piracy
3. Nepotism, compromising one's position, good ol' boy/girl networks
4. Fudging or cooking the data in research or analysis
5. Working on or with weapons or espionage systems
6. Keeping quiet because it's not your problem (Wujek 1989)

Email Ethics Issues

Here are some good email rules to consider (Brenner, 2005):

- Denial—Do not indicate that you did not read or receive a message if you really did.
- Abusive omission—Do not exclude someone on an outgoing email just because you do not like them.
- Misidentifying yourself—It may be ethical to hide your identity, but it is not right to mislead readers that you are someone else.
- Dragging your feet—Do not make a person wait for your email reply, misstating that you didn't get or see their email as early as you really did.

- Wandering eyes—Do not read other people's email unless you are invited to, even if it accidentally comes to you.
- Forgery—Do not change emails that you are forwarding if it alters the intention of the original sender.

And remember that netiquette strictly forbids ever sending any kind of a negative email. Have the courage to address someone in person, or at least over the telephone, if you have something less than positive to communicate to them. And if someone sends you a negative email, do not reply via email to them. Ignore it, go see them, or call them.

Reacting to Unethical Requests

What happens when your supervisor asks or orders you to do something that may be unethical or even illegal? We are placed in a crossfire situation where we want to obey our boss, yet from a moral perspective, the order goes against our personal beliefs or standards. Here are some suggestions to consider before you respond to your boss.

1. Make sure that what you are being asked to do is actually wrong. If you think the matter is legally incorrect, make sure you understand the law before jumping to any conclusions. If it is an ethical or moral matter, consult with someone more knowledgeable and experienced since ethical issues can be quite complicated. Seek out someone you respect with regard to the matter such as a lawyer or someone with expertise in the related field.

2. Just because your boss asked you at one time to do something that you considered ethically inappropriate, try to keep from labeling him or her in your mind as generally unethical. Your boss is still the boss and your responsibility as an employee is to treat him or her with the utmost respect. Entertain all his or her future requests with a completely open mind.

3. Your employer may have a good reason for asking you to do something that you consider unethical. Consider other ethical or legal alternatives and suggest them to your boss, or try sharing your specific concerns in a non-threatening way.

4. If you do discover that there is another more ethical alternative to solve your employer's request, appeal to your employer's sense of right and wrong. Explain that your solution removes any concern about possible legal penalties or fines. If possible, stress that you are committed to the company and make it clear that the final decision is his or hers, not yours.

5. If you cannot come up with a viable alternative plan, be prepared to receive criticism or accusations of disloyalty for doing what you believe is the right thing. Explain to your boss that you are not comfortable participating in the given activity. In some cases, you may not even want to be identified with the business and you may be forced to resign.

    Taking a stand for your own convictions may cost you a promotion or even your job; obedience to doing the honorable and right things can translate to a meaningful loss in income. Remember that to many employers and to your peers, your commitment to do the right thing may appear foolish. Yet, violating your personal, ethical, and moral code could be even more devastating to you (adapted from Abbot, 1986).

Whistleblowing

Whistleblowing is when you make known to the public facts and opinions that you believe are in the public's best interests. You are telling on the company, or letting the cat out of the bag. This should be the last alternative, a step you will hopefully never have to take. Whistleblowing may carry a disparaging connotation, and is sometimes done for self-serving purposes. In the *ideal* case, however, it is no more than acting ethically (and professionally) (Wujek 1989).

Ethics Scenarios

The following scenarios are a few true accounts of experiences reported by past new professionals.

"My boss asked me to copy some licensed software onto five other computers that did not have licenses for the software."

"Throughout my job, I sensed a sort of apathy among the employees. There were a few that were very diligent and hard working, but the majority of the employees didn't seem to care much. It was as if you were looked down upon if you were a hard worker. This to me is not how an organization should be run and I think it stemmed from the fact that an employee in our kind of business is almost impossible to fire. So there was no fear of losing one's job. Therefore, why work hard?"

"Working for an insurance broker, my boss asked me to call a number of our competitors, lie about my name, tell them that I was a college student working on a paper, and ask them to mail me some particular reports of an otherwise confidential nature."

"My sole job was to call our competing companies, as if I were a potential customer, and ask them questions about their products."

"I learned that it was common practice that if a chemical tank was out of spec, the tester would use the results of the day before and throw some chemicals in the tank and everything would be okay by tomorrow. It was also not unusual to step on the scales of the stress machine to ensure the recording needle logged the sample as passing. I found it greatly disturbing having to be involved with this mode of operation."

"I was frustrated working with the boss's son, as he only carried half his load."

"I had been putting in a lot of overtime on the job when one day, my supervisor, who was very high up in the company, told me to take my wife out to a nice dinner and show, and to charge it to the company as a business expense. I wanted to accept his 'token of appreciation,' but didn't feel right."

"I applied for a permanent position with a firm without telling them that I was only temporarily available and that I would be quitting after six months."

OFFICE POLITICS

Office politics means different things to different people. For most, the immediate connotation is negative, unethical, cheap, debasing, unprofessional, lowly, weak, and nasty. The word "politics" by itself often conjures up a negative connotation.

So what are office politics? And perhaps more usefully, what is it REALLY? Consider some of the following, contradictory responses from more seasoned professionals:

Definitions of Office Politics

- The old practice in the workplace of doing things just for the sake of self-promotion.
- Making short-term compromises for the sake of long-term gains.
- Game-playing that seeks to enhance one's own image, or denigrate that of a colleague who may offer some threat to you. It tends to be confined to specific areas of a company for each given person, but it is found at all levels.
- It includes activities such as getting in and keeping in good graces with people above and below you through means outside of simply doing your work well.
- Going to extra efforts to be seen working, such as attending the boss's Christmas party.
- Bad-mouthing people above you in order to buoy your own image.

Office politics clearly carries different meanings for different people. It is a term that is not necessarily heard often in most work environments. It seems to be referenced more to management types of professionals who have significant decision-making authority, who have to please a lot of people, and who have a lot of people who have to please them.

Is it good, or is it bad?

You have to accept that there is likely to be some level of office politics wherever you go. For example, the person at the top is always going to seem to have his or her favorites. Interviews with myriad seasoned professionals show they largely agree that although office politics carries a stigma, it is to some extent a necessary part of game-playing, and can have ultimate positive outcomes (funny as that may sound—but keep reading!). My interviews with these people also agree that:

> **Office politics is a bad thing when people cross the ethical and professional lines of integrity, doing or saying unkind things about other people, or making inappropriate compromises.**

So, office politics can mean figuring out how to give people what they want without compromising your personal ethics. It might mean yielding a net positive gain for your company and society, at the cost of a generally benign or lesser compromise.

Many argue that it is in fact incumbent upon a manager to engage in office politics, again, stopping short of doing anything that is too inappropriate. Image is important. We want and need to be viewed as the just and good soldier, rather than dog-eat-dog like.

When office politics appear to cross the line of appropriate compromises, they can decrease overall personal enjoyment, fulfillment, and productivity. While different personalities will always exist on a team (TEAM: Together Everybody Accomplishes More), and different personal chemistries will be more compatible than others, perceived over-compromises go a step beyond these realities. Unfair treatment is wrong and scorned by all. (Incidentally, these political-appearing behaviors are not confined to the workplace. Churches, service clubs, Little League, etc., abound in such actions as people try to get things their own way.)

If you are a good manager, moving the company forward, you might give an honor to a board member who was less than deserving, but who would in turn make a large contribution to the company. Is this ethical? How much has anybody been hurt? Did everybody benefit overall, ultimately? Perhaps it is in everybody's greatest overall interest to do something special for one person who can in turn do something extremely valuable for everybody else?

The image is not always reality. You read about a politician's relative winning a contract from the government, and you imagine something sneaky going on behind the scenes. But sometimes there are understandable explanations.

The following are specific suggestions offered by current practicing professionals. Keep in mind that since professionals differ widely in their opinions on this matter, many of the following suggestions conflict:

> "Study the company organizational chart. Know who carries what kind of rank or clout."

> "You need to strike a balance between the 'purist' and the 'politician.'"

> "Students sometimes leave their school environment and are too quick to try to prove themselves and get the next promotion. Start off working hard, but moderate the visibility of your efforts. Stay low for a while."

"Get involved. Be visible. Don't run away from office politics, because you will just run into it someplace else."

"Develop a long-term goal and game plan for attaining your goals, but not 'at all costs.' You must have standards, even if you must move on to another job to live by them."

"Don't be too fast or too aggressive."

"Don't work for the next job. Do a good job in the one you are in. You don't know who or when, but someone is watching who will recognize you and promote you."

"You must play the rules of the game in your institution."

"In the long run, you must develop 'political clout' if you really want to make a difference and be able to effect positive change."

"Butt-kissing is very prevalent. You can't get away from it. It is still extremely disdainful. I refuse to stoop to it myself."

"Practice diplomacy."

"Self-confidence is an important virtue. Without tact, it comes across as arrogance."

"You need to learn to 'manage up.' The tendency is to manage down, i.e., just doing your job well and making sure everything below you goes well. You also have to present yourself to people above you to know what a good job you are doing. It can't be enough to just know you did a good job."

"Take jobs outside your forte that will increase your exposure and be more likely to advance your career."

"Nobody likes a twenty-two-year-old know-it-all. Do not convey an attitude of being above doing certain jobs."

"The last thing line employees want is to have a new college graduate telling them how to do their jobs. Exercise the greatest of tact."

"Realize that the real world is not always like the textbook said it would be. Realities sometimes dictate open-mindedness."

A FEW MORE IDEAS ON DISCRETION IN GENERAL

1. Be slow to share personal business and personal information at work. Keep your discussions more professional and superficial. If you develop more personal relationships with colleagues, continue to move slowly in divulging too much personal information. This includes with your supervisor.
2. Do not bring romantic problems to work. (Easier said than done sometimes.)
3. Be careful about spending time at work planning personal activities (e.g., vacations, weddings, and birthdays).
4. Offer to rearrange your schedule when necessary.
5. Personal friends should not come to see you at work unless you are **110% SURE!** that it is okay with your supervisor. If it is okay, then the visits should be kept to a minimum. If they begin to stay too long, just tell them you need to get back to work.
6. Your husband/wife/boyfriend/girlfriend should be very careful with how much they come to your office, distracting you from your work. On the other hand, an occasional appearance showing their love for you and support of your work can be *very* positive. And it's extremely important that they support company parties with their presence when families are invited.

7. If you have children, they should not come into the office but for rare and extremely brief personal visits or business with you.

8. Do not turn on music (or listen to music using headphones) unless you are positive this is okay with your supervisor.

9. Be sensitive to office mates who may be within earshot of you. Potential desk rage triggers are serial gum-snapping, poor cell phone and text-messaging etiquette, annoying cell phone ring tones, loud frequent pen-clicking, snorting sounds, loud keyboard tapping (don't be a keyboard assaultist), yelling out the time every hour as a deadline approaches, and smelly lunches. (Kitchen 2007)

10. Do not bring any food into the office that is unwrapped. Beverages at your desk may be okay, as long as you are cautious about not placing them near any work that could be ruined by them.

11. You may be exposed to records of a confidential nature. Avoid any unnecessary contact with or exposure to these matters, and exercise extreme discretion with discussing these materials or your related work. **Never look up anything in any of these files for personal reasons.**

12. Understand workplace culture—When in Rome, do as the Romans do.

13. Be involved with, and take advantage of, events the company puts on.

14. Personal use of office phones, computers, copy machines, etc., should be kept to a minimum, including personal emails. This is worth asking your supervisor about explicitly.

15. Avoid use of your email and Instant Messenger programs for non-work purposes. As with all these things, just check with your supervisor regarding company policies and practices.

16. Basic common manners go a long way.

17. Keep your chin up.

18. If in doubt, just ask.

19. Benefit from praise and criticism. Respond well to feedback.
20. Learn from mistakes. Make fresh ones, not the same ones.
21. Be honest. Always. In every way.

Here is the best recommendation of the whole book. This may be the hardest thing you ever attempt to do. I doubt there has ever been a person in the history of the world who wasn't glad they did it. Or that anybody has ever regretted doing it. Are you ready?

If a person upsets you strongly in some way,
sleep on it at least one night before responding.

You can go so far as typing up an email to the person, but do not press Send until the next day. Maybe even press "Delete." Like the bumper sticker says, "Don't do it."

In conclusion, I strongly encourage you to find a mentor. Identify and approach at least one person who has had similar experiences as you are having, and of course whom you respect for their wisdom and intelligence. Take them to lunch once in a while and just discuss specific and general aspects of your career, personal responsibilities, where you have been, and where you are going. You will grow in wisdom and stature yourself. You will exercise much better discretion.

Principle

1   2   3   4   **5**   6   7

Practice Good
Communication Skills

THE SINGLE MOST IMPORTANT SKILL

Your ability to communicate is the single most important skill that will determine whether or not you get hired for each job you apply for and, once you are on the job, how successful you will be. Your speaking and writing are constantly judged by all who come into contact with them, both at work and in leisure settings. Something as simple as a poorly written email can tarnish your image. A design, marketing, or sales report that is sloppy, unorganized, and loaded with spelling errors tells the reader that you are sloppy, unorganized, and loaded with errors.

Communications are everywhere in any job. Some corporate professionals recently brainstormed the following when asked what the writing requirements are for their job:

daily short emails	justifications	response time reports	problem reports
progress reports	performance evaluations	faxes	pass-downs
letters	specs	software bulletins	technical papers
minutes	proposals	requests for action	technical articles
status reports	procedures	bug reports	invoice rejections
period reports	change notices	purchase orders	
trip reports	requests for quotations	reliability reports	

When asked what comes to their minds when they think about writing requirements of the job, they listed:

Good
satisfaction
completeness
quick
structure
organized
joy

Bad
confusion
fear
boredom
frustration
indifference
tension
unhappy
how to start
lost
depressed
headache

A comparison in the size of this list verifies the importance of addressing this subject.

While there are a number of things you can do to improve your communication skills, perhaps the first and most important step is to adopt an *attitude* of excellence in communication. As employers' needs and concerns for excellent communication skills have grown, more authors are now offering enjoyable, interesting, and entertaining books on the topic. Go to your local bookstore and pick one up that interests you, and read a few pages every day. Consider it a personal development exercise. College English and grammar textbooks can also add to your arsenal of resource books for professional communication, strange as that might sound. (I recommend *The Elements of Style* by Strunk and White and *Write Right!* by Jan Venolia.)

The rest of this chapter offers some simple and specific ideas for improving your writing and verbal skills for use on the job.

THE POWER OF THE TONGUE

What you say and how you say it can either mark you as an intelligent, confident, persuasive, and professional, or as insensitive, lacking forethought, and obtuse. You may have already taken a speech class that has discussed some of the basics of effective communication. Some of these guidelines are

1. **Maintain good eye contact**. But don't stare the person down. In some cultures, looking someone in the eyes too strongly while speaking is considered disrespectful. Watch for cultural differences that can interfere with effective verbal communication.
2. **Watch your body language**. Stand or sit somewhat erect with a somewhat open posture. But don't do either to an extreme. You want to show interest and self-confidence, stopping short of exuding aggressiveness or arrogance.

    Note that the distance between you and the listener (called "personal space") will vary greatly from culture to culture. Americans and some Europeans speak to each other standing fairly closely, about an arm's length away. If someone keeps backing away from you, honor and respect this move.

3. **Watch your temper**. Stay calm, cool, and collected. This is always impressive to other people, and it's good for your health. Do not humiliate or demean others. If someone has done something to offend you or anger you, do not respond immediately (see Discretion chapter). Take up your differences in private and control your anger. Managers who use anger as a way to control their staff develop not only fear but also contempt and hatred on the part of their support personnel. Foul language also has no place in a business and professional environment. At school, it is sometimes considered acceptable or even the norm to use this type of language. But in the professional world, it frequently turns people off. Look for more creative and intellectual ways to express your feelings and observations.

4. **Avoid sexist comments**. Most people today are very sensitive to language and jokes that imply any kind of female or male disparagement. The sexist professional barriers are slowly coming down, but there is still much work to be done. Sexual harassment charges abound, and consequently have seemed to become a joking matter in many workplaces. Don't go there. Don't even laugh.

5. **Avoid racist comments**. Just like sexism, don't go there. Big big big mistake.

6. **Avoid all other insensitive comments as well**. You might be surprised how often you say things that are offensive to different populations. This can include people of different physical and intellectual capabilities, gender identification, sexual orientation, and many other areas. Strive for increased understanding and humane decorum.

7. **Polite AND confident**. These sound like contradictory terms, but both should be goals of the new professional. Barbara Pachter, a career coach, suggests:

   ○ "Cut out words like 'kinda' and 'sorta' and 'maybe.' Because you know, um, if you use those words, you kinda sound sorta like you don't really believe in what you're saying. Maybe. Dude."
   ○ "Don't speak too softly. You can become invisible and easy to over-look." (2000)

CRACK THE DICTIONARY AND PROOFREAD YOUR WORK

Proofing—Computers do ninety percent of the work for you. Yet, so many professionals don't want to take the extra minute to review the words that have been highlighted by the spell and grammar checker. Typos can impair the reader's comprehension of your work. But at a minimum, they mar your image. Even those three-sentence emails are important.

Proofreading is tedious, and often feels unnecessary. We tend to feel like the job is done once we type the last paragraph of a document. Consider the job to *not* be complete until you have proofread your work. Read it all the way through, including catching the spell-checker highlights.

Revise—The more important documents require your very best writing. These can be more like masterpieces that you need to reread and revise numerous times, striving for clarity, cleanliness, organization, and conciseness. [Malcolm Forbes gives the advice, "search out and annihilate all unnecessary words and sentences—even entire paragraphs" (Baldrige 1985, 100)]. Write tight.

GENERAL COMMUNICATION MISTAKES

1. Not giving enough information;
2. Getting information or instructions to or from the wrong person in the communication or decision-making chain;
3. Giving out information prematurely;
4. Using written communication instead of oral communication (and vice versa);

   Rule of three emails: If you expect that you will need to have three or more email exchanges with a person to deal with a matter, you should pick up the phone and call the person instead.

5. Speaking too softly or unclearly. Speaking too quietly can convey timidity, a lack of enthusiasm, and/or a lack of self-confidence. It also obviously hampers communication at its most basic level.

BUSINESS-WORLD VOCABULARY, JARGON AND EXPRESSIONS

Of the many skills that will enhance your professional work performance, your vernacular plays an integral role. All professionals must dedicate themselves to a life-long pursuit of expanding their vocabulary and generally improving their written and oral communication skills.

The richer your vocabulary, the better your ability to understand communications, and to express yourself. There is in fact a theory that the more words you possess in your vocabulary, the greater your ability to think.

After years of being forced to look up words and write down their definitions over and over again in school, it is no wonder that most of us choose not to once we graduate. But this can be invaluable personal development. I have an expectation of myself to look up at least one word every day. I have dictionary.com on my cell and tablet. So it just takes a second to bring up the word. I look up only words that I generally recognize, or otherwise feel like I *should* know. And then I usually add it to my Favorites list in the program, so that once in a while, I can review that list and test my memory. I come across such a word nearly every day from reading periodicals, novels, and other works.

Another great investment is the *Pimsleur Verbal Advantage* CDs. The speaker is a former Harvard professor who introduces words that are just above the average user's vocabulary. He does an excellent job of keeping the sessions fairly interesting and entertaining, periodically interjecting fun grammar lessons.

Author Letitia Baldrige writes:

> If you think of another executive as having a good voice, you may or may not be aware that his choice of words also influences how you regard the sound of his voice. A good vocabulary helps a person to make good conversation and to communicate well; it also affects the quality of one's voice affirmatively.
>
> The English language has many beautiful sounds. An executive who uses a word like "mellifluous," for example, must make an effort to pronounce it properly. It is a beautiful word, evoking a pleasant image. An enriched vocabulary sounds good to the ear and lends attractiveness to a voice. A person who uses distinguished words properly, sounds distinguished and makes you want to listen to him (1985, 65).

Many successful professionals in the business world color their formal and informal speech with expressions and sayings, especially in the forms of similes and metaphors. (See examples below.) You might find it helpful to note some of these expressions and to start working them into your own professional speech. (See Appendix D.)

Common Expressions

Put to bed: To complete a matter; to settle (as in sending a newspaper to print).

Between a rock and a hard spot: A predicament wherein none of the alternatives will work; bad effect whatever you do.

To bite the bullet: To consent to doing something difficult or undesirable, often for a longer-term gain. (Orig.: People used to bite down on bullets during surgery to relieve some of the stress and pain before the days of anesthesia.)

Fast lane: Implies much action, excitement, and perhaps stress associated with something.

Honeymoon period: Period of time immediately following a new union such as when you go to work for a new company. Usually accompanied by higher tolerance, flexibility, and possibly a more evaluating eye.

More Sophisticated Expressions

To compare apples and oranges: To compare two things that are difficult to compare due to differences in their constitution or make-up, as are apples and oranges. You just cannot compare them.

Bargaining chip: A potential concession to be used for another gain.

To look at something with blinders: Not to look at or consider the whole picture or all the options. (Orig.: Racehorses are outfitted with blinders to keep them from being distracted during a race.)

Bottom line: The result, what is left, after all is said and done. The product. (Orig.: Financial term referring to the total cost or the profit at the end of a project's term or period.)

Have a chip on one's shoulder: Angry (ready to fight) with someone. Being on the defensive. (Orig.: A boy puts a stick on his shoulder and dares another boy to knock it off. If he does knock it off, then he is accepting a challenge to fight.)

To cut one's teeth on something: To gain experience on that something during young or formative years. For example, Kids are cutting their teeth on the Internet.

Pays high dividends: Very beneficial. Indicates high worth, reward, and/or payoff for a given effort or other type of investment.

Fielder's choice: To make a decision between equally effective options. (Orig.: In baseball, a fielder can sometimes throw out one of two different runners without a significant difference in the overall consequence.)

Shoot from the hip: To do or say something without being prepared or ready, as a gunfighter might shoot when his gun is by his hip rather than raising his gun all the way up and taking careful aim.

To get in the trenches: To go to where the action or work is actually taking place, the site of execution. Negative connotation if a person has never been in the trenches. (Orig.: Refers to soldiers in the trenches of the war frontlines.)

Principle

$$1 \quad 2 \quad 3 \quad 4 \quad 5 \quad \boxed{6} \quad 7$$

Optimize Your Time Management

When seasoned professionals review this book, they frequently comment that even *they* found this section helpful. Personal productivity and efficiency have become such strong sciences that most people can benefit by at least reviewing the following principles occasionally. Good time management boils down largely to working smart. The most productive people operate under the strictest codes of setting priorities and living by them. They put one hundred percent into everything they do, whether it is solving a problem at work, training at the gym, or taking a break. "Focus" is their middle name. They strive for balance. And they set their sights on outcomes.

Living by priorities inherently means learning to say "no" to countless requests. **To say 'yes' to one thing is to say 'no' to another.** (Think about it.) Or another way to view this is, "To 'stretch yourself too thin' is to compromise your priorities." Nobody likes to disappoint other people by having to say no, but again, good time managers will protect their higher priorities.

The science of Time Management consists predominantly of countless specific tips. Consequently, I shall present the majority of this chapter in the form of bullets and lists. Remember that you are an individual; you are unique. You can learn from others, but you should do what works best for you.

TIME WASTERS AND SAVERS

The following is a list of some of the most common Time Wasters and Time Savers suggested by a cross-section of business executives.

Time Wasters

1. Unnecessary paperwork
2. Clutter
3. Excessive record-keeping
4. Unclear communication
5. Indecisiveness
6. Poorly planned meetings
7. Telephone calls that last too long
8. Mental blocks
9. Perfectionism
10. Backlogs of unfinished projects

Time Savers

1. Goal setting and goal making, as well as keeping deadlines
2. Setting priorities for tasks, goals, and projects
3. Saying no to protect and preserve your priorities
4. Establishing routines
5. Delegating responsibility
6. Segmenting (breaking up into manageable parts) large tasks
7. Concentrating on one thing at a time
8. Keeping a follow-up file and referring to it on a regular basis

TIME MANAGEMENT: A COLLECTION OF INDIVIDUAL RESPONSES

I collect responses from people to the question, "What are your Time Management tricks?" While I do not necessarily subscribe to all of the following, these are the ones I find at least bear reporting.

1. I listen to NPR (National Public Radio) when I am driving, and I listen to audiobooks when I am exercising.
2. I count all my time as on-time and try to get satisfaction (not necessarily accomplishment) out of every minute.
3. I try to enjoy whatever I am doing.
4. I am a perennial optimist.
5. I build on successes.
6. I don't waste time regretting my failures.
7. I don't waste my time feeling guilty about what I don't do.
8. I remind myself: There is always enough time for the important things. If it is important, I will make the time to do it.
9. I get up at 5 a.m. during the week (and I go to bed early).
10. "To be early is to be on time. To be on time is to be late."
11. I don't carve my to-do list in stone—I try to remain flexible.
12. I have a light lunch so I don't get sleepy in the afternoon.
13. I don't read newspapers or magazines very thoroughly.
14. I skim books quickly looking for ideas.
15. I don't own a television set.
16. I have my home close to my office.
17. I examine old habits for possible elimination or streamlining.
18. I have given up forever all waiting time. If I have to wait, I consider it a gift of time to relax, plan, or do something I would not otherwise have done.
19. I keep my watch three minutes fast to get a head start on everything.

20. I jot down notes on my smart phone when I think of things important to remember.
21. I revise my lifetime goal list once a month.
22. I review my lifetime goal list every day and identify activities to do each day to further my goals.
23. I put signs in my office reminding me of my goals.
24. I keep my long-term goals in mind even while doing the smallest task.
25. I always plan first thing in the morning and set priorities for the day.
26. I schedule actual appointments in my calendar for working on specific assignments.
27. I keep a list of specific items to be done each day, arrange them in priority order, and then do my best to get the important ones done as soon as possible.
28. I schedule my time months in advance in such a way that each month offers variety and balance, as well as open time reserved for hot projects.
29. I give myself time off and special rewards when I have done the important things.
30. I do first things first.
31. I work smarter rather than harder.
32. I try to do only A's, never B's or C's.
33. I have confidence in my judgment of priorities and stick to them in spite of difficulties.
34. I ask myself, "Would anything terrible happen if I didn't do this priority item?" If the answer is no, I don't do it.
35. If I seem to procrastinate, I ask myself, "What am I avoiding?" Then I try to confront that thing head-on.
36. I always use the 80/20 rule. (Most people spend eighty percent of their time doing low-priority items, and twenty percent doing high-priority items. The 80/20 rule reverses this.)
37. I start with the most profitable parts of large projects and often find it not necessary to do the rest.

38. I cut off nonproductive activities as quickly as possible.
39. I give myself enough time to concentrate on high-priority items.
40. I have developed the ability to concentrate well for long stretches of time, sometimes with the aid of coffee. (Starbucks employees know my name.)
41. I concentrate on one thing at a time.
42. I focus my efforts on items that will have the best long-term benefits.
43. I keep pushing, and am persistent when I sense I have a winner.
44. I have trained myself to go down my to-do list without skipping over the difficult items.
45. I do much of my thinking on paper.
46. I do work alone creatively in the morning and use the afternoon for meetings, if necessary.
47. I set deadlines for others and myself.
48. I try to listen actively in every discussion.
49. I try not to waste other people's time (unless it is something that really matters to me).
50. I delegate everything I possibly can to others.
51. I make use of specialists to help me with special problems.
52. I have someone screen my email and phone calls and handle all routine matters.
53. I generate as little paperwork as possible and throw away anything I possibly can.
54. I handle each piece of paper only once.
55. I keep my desktop cleared for action, and put the most important thing in the center of my desk.
56. I have a place for everything (so I waste as little time as possible looking for things).
57. I try not to think of work on weekends.
58. I relax and do nothing rather frequently.
59. I recognize that inevitably some of my time will be spent on activities outside my control and don't fret about it.

60. I keep small talk to a minimum during work hours.
61. I look for action steps to be taken now to further my goals.
62. I am continually asking myself, "What is the best use of my time right now?"
63. I use the Swiss cheese method when I am avoiding something, by breaking it into smaller tasks and just doing one of the smaller tasks for fifteen minutes.
64. I practice the art of intelligent neglect, eliminating trivial tasks from my life as much as possible.
65. I look ahead in my month and try to anticipate what is going to happen so I can better schedule my time.
66. I manage the amount of time I spend in meetings. I find out which ones are mandatory or really important. I sometimes skip meetings if it might be more valuable to complete an assignment.
67. I note deadlines in my calendar, and I add a second note a few days before the deadline reminding me it's coming.
68. I try to be an optimist and seek out the good in my life.
69. I take breaks as reward for work. Not only are the breaks good motivation to help me complete something, I also am more refreshed to tackle the next bit of work after a break.

KEY POINTS FROM VARIOUS STUDIES ON TIME MANAGEMENT

1. Getting less than eight hours of rest seriously compromises our ability to concentrate and solve problems.
2. Creativity rarely strikes in a flash, but more typically results from steady cogitation.
3. Multitasking, for all its seeming efficiency, can exact a heavy toll on the quality of our output.
4. Daily meditation physically transforms the cerebral cortex.

5. Physical exercise may be as important as mental gymnastics in keeping Alzheimer's disease at bay.
6. The human brain retains an astonishing degree of plasticity and capacity for learning throughout life. Doesn't peak until midlife.
7. Don't stress too much; relaxation is a balm for the overtaxed brain.
8. Dangerous attitudes:
   a. "I never do just two things at once if I can possibly do four or five."
   b. "I feel anxious when my in-box is full; but I feel no better when it is empty."
9. Dr. Edward Hallowell, a psychiatrist in Sudbury, Massachusetts, and author of best-selling books, including *Driven to Distraction* and *Overbooked and About to Snap: Strategies for Coping in a World Gone ADD.*
   a. Has seen a tenfold rise in the number of patients showing up with symptoms that closely resemble those of attention-deficit disorder (ADD), but of a work-induced variety. Attributes this to attempts by working professionals to multitask.
      i. More irritable.
      ii. Productivity declining.
      iii. Couldn't get organized.
      iv. Making decisions in black-and-white, shoot-from-the-hip ways due to pressure to get things done quickly.
      v. Leads to distractibility, impulsiveness and haste, guilt, and inadequacy.
   b. Recommendations
      i. Prioritize ruthlessly
      ii. Cultivate the lilies or the things that fulfill you.
      iii. Cut the leeches, those that deplete you.

        iv. Allot thirty minutes a day for thinking, relaxing or meditating.

        v. Get significant doses of "Vitamin C": the live Connection to other people.

10. Multitasker's Glossary

    a. Screen sucking—Wasting time online long after you have finished what you signed on to do.

    b. Frazzing—Frantic, ineffective multitasking, typically with the delusion that you are getting a lot done.

    c. Pizzled—How you feel when someone you're with pulls out a cell phone and uses it without an explanation or apology. (Cross between p_____ off and puzzled.)

    d. Doomdart—The internal distraction of a forgotten task that pops into your mind when you are doing something else. A side effect of frazzing.

11. Report entitled *The Cost of Not Paying Attn.* (Basex, an information-technology research firm in NY)

    a. Interruptions now consume an average of 2.1 hours a day, or 28% of the workday.

    b. This includes the recovery time associated with getting back on task.

    c. Workplace interruptions cost the U.S. economy $588 billion per year.

    d. Biggest causes of interruptions in descending order

        i. Colleague stops by

        ii. Being called away from the desk

        iii. Arrival of new email: Fifty-five percent of workers open email immediately or shortly after it arrives, no matter how busy they are. Most people don't even think about turning off the dinger.

        iv. Switching to another task on the computer

        v. Phone call

12. Research shows breakfast provides the day's most vital brain food.
13. Keep cell phones and iPods off or away when in transit so you can use the downtime for thinking.
14. How racehorses win: They come out of gate with blinders on and go for the finish line. They don't care what the competition is doing.
15. Some companies give employees Do not interrupt signs to put up as needed.
16. Scientists used to think intellectual power peaked at age forty. Hooey!
    a. Brain brings new cognitive systems online and cross-indexes existing ones as you get older.
    b. Short- and long-term memory may not be as strong, but you manage info and parse meanings better.
    c. Women's highest inductive reasoning abilities range from ages forty to early sixties. (Presumably similar for men?)
17. Athlete Paradigm
    a. Athletes talk a lot about getting in and staying in the zone.
        i. Magical place where mind and body work in perfect synch and movements seem to flow without conscious effort
        ii. Athletic nirvana
    b. Set-backs (From Michael Johnson—Olympic sprinter)
        i. "If you have disappointments, you need to ask yourself 'Why did I not perform well today? Was it the preparation? A mistake in execution?' Then you need to get yourself at peace with that situation."
        ii. "Achieving that peace is the key to avoiding a full-fledged slump—that downward spiral that only gets worse the harder you try."

    c. Training is about strengthening the mind–body connection. Athletes need to train their mind with the same discipline that they train their bodies.

    d. One way experts help athletes control the jitters is by teaching them to take command of the interior monologues that psychologists call self-talk.

        i. This is the endless conversation that we all have with ourselves, processing events as they pass before our eyes.

        ii. The average person speaks to himself at a rate of 300–1,000 words a minute.

        iii. You must replace any negative self-talk with positive self-talk.

    e. The first thing an athlete has to realize is that he or she always in control.

18. Sleeping your way to the top

    a. Eight hours/night; nine for adolescents; seventy-one percent of American adults and eighty-five percent of teens do not get this

    b. Purpose is more to rest the mind than the body

    c. Helps consolidate memory, improve judgment, promote learning and concentration, boost mood, speed reaction time and sharpen problem-solving and accuracy

    d. Wake up each day at the same time; but if you need extra rest, sleep late on Saturday rather than Sunday, because that way the work week won't start with Monday morning blues.

    e. Avoid late-night snacks and alcohol, since digestion prevents quality rest

    f. Exercising early in the morning increases the risk of injury since the body is not warmed up and is less coordinated; too late at night may keep you from falling asleep quickly

19. Creativity
   a. Many people believe creativity comes in a sudden moment of insight and that this magical burst of an idea is a different mental process from everyday thinking. Not true. Just uses same building blocks you use every day—like when you figure out a way around a traffic jam.
   b. Three B's—bathtub, bed, and bus—places where ideas have emerged. When we take time off from working on a problem, and we change what we're doing and our context, that can activate different areas of our brain. If the answer is not in the part of the brain we were using, it might be in another.
   c. People who are creative have tons of ideas, many of them bad. But even bad ideas can be useful.
   d. Take risks and expect to make lots of mistakes. Creativity is a numbers game. Work hard and take frequent breaks, but stay with it over time. Do what you love, because creative breakthroughs take years of hard work.
   e. Develop a network of colleagues.
   f. Schedule time for freewheeling.
   g. Forget romantic myths that creativity is all about being artsy and gifted.
   h. Other myths. Creative people
      i. get a great idea in a flash and then execute it
      ii. always have great ideas
      iii. have radical new ideas that come out of nowhere
      iv. blindly ignore convention because their inspiration springs full-blown from their subconscious
20. Meditation
   a. Scientists find that meditation not only reduces stress but also reshapes the brain.
   b. Some evidence that the daily practice of meditation increases attention span, sharpens focus, and improves memory.

    c. Seems to help regulate emotions, which in turn helps people get along—emotional intelligence.

21. Caffeine

    a. Makes more alert, focused, quick-witted, clever. Enhances short-term memory. Improves reaction time and mental acuity. (Wellness Letter, 2013)

    b. Appears to have some protective effect against liver damage, Parkinson's disease, diabetes, Alzheimer's, gallstones, depression, and maybe even some forms of cancer.

    c. Only proven medical down side appears to be a temporary elevation in blood pressure, which is a problem only if you already suffer from hypertension. Small evidence also for miscarriage and benign breast cysts, but this is highly controversial.

    d. If well rested, tends to improve rudimentary brain functions, like keeping your attention focused on boring, repetitive tasks for long periods. Also tends to improve mood, and makes people feel more energetic.

    e. When sleep-deprived and you take caffeine, pretty much anything you measure will improve: reaction time, vigilance, attention, logical reasoning, most of the complex functions you associate with intelligence (remember that most Americans are sleep-deprived most of the time) (*Time* 2006).

STRIKING A BALANCE BETWEEN YOUR PROFESSIONAL AND PERSONAL GOALS

This may be the most important subject in this book. The old question of, "Are you living to work or working to live?" depicts the range in values and attitudes different individuals live out. Are you working as hard as you should to increase your job and financial security? Are you taking good care of your body? Are you being a good family member and friend? Are you making a positive difference in the world? And are you having some fun along the way? Senior citizens frequently reflect back on their lives with such comments as wishing they could do it again, so that they could put *more* time in one of these areas, or *less* in another. So how do you look at the big picture to set, and live out, your priorities? This is called work–life balance.

Jack Welch, former CEO for General Electric (GE) wrote a book called *Winning*, in which he makes three suggestions regarding work–life balance:

1. Focus on the task at hand. If you are at work, focus on your work, and do not do such personal things as plan family vacations. When you are home, focus on your family or personal things. Do not conduct business phone calls in the middle of your golf game.
2. Say no to opportunities outside your work–life plan. If your plan calls for taking your spouse out for dinner every Tuesday evening, do not allow other opportunities that may arise to challenge this commitment.
3. Take care of yourself, including rest, exercise, and fun. (2007)

A healthy work–life balance optimizes your overall fulfillment. It also contributes immediately to your productivity.

So after determining the broader parameters for yourself, such as how many hours you should work each week, a subsequent important key is learning to make the best possible use of the time that is left over. Many students work so hard during their school years that they do not feel like they have very much free time. And it is sort of chopped up, rather than existing in solid blocks of time. Working professionals have lives that are quite different from the world of school. Their lives tend to revolve around an eight- to nine-hour workday, with evenings and weekends off. More dedicated employees may spend much more time on work, leaving that much less time available in the balance. Regardless, how do you get the most of this remaining leisure time?

Your leisure time presents an invaluable opportunity for personal growth, increased health, and overall happiness and fulfillment. You should approach the question of how to use your spare time like you'd approach any topic of importance in your life. That means taking the time to consider what you'd like to do in a constructive manner. Ask yourself:

What are the other priorities in my life outside of my career?
What would I like to get out of my leisure time?

Some obvious examples are regular physical conditioning, pleasure reading, intellectual stimulation, and maintaining personal relationships with family and friends.

Sit down and think about it. Brainstorm on a sheet of paper some of the ideas that come to mind. Maybe even ask some friends what they do with their leisure time that is important to them. Think about which ones are realistic and affordable. Whatever you come up with, write it down someplace. If you keep any kind of a personal journal, that might be a good place to record it. If your goals can be measurable, you will enjoy looking back over your journal entries over time to see how you did.

INTELLECTUAL IDEAS FOR YOUR SPARE TIME

1. Read or at least skim:
   a. Job-related texts or manuals
   b. Professional journals
   c. Periodicals such as the *Wall Street Journal*, *Newsweek*, or your local daily newspaper
2. Take an evening class
   a. On financial planning
   b. Related to your job
   c. About something that just interests you
3. Look into graduate programs
4. Tutor local high school students
5. Learn a new language
6. Join a professional society/organization
7. Professional registration preparation (e.g., EIT—Engineering in Training exam)
8. Write research paper on a subject of interest
9. Travel more

Be interesting!

In order to be interesting, you have to do interesting things. You only go around once in life, so take advantage of it. Travel to other countries. Try different parties. Accept unique challenges. Don't do anything that is dangerous, but the only way you can have interesting things to share at Thanksgiving is if you do things out of the ordinary. So don't be boring—be interesting!

This is the shortest chapter in the book, but again, it may be the most important. The level of success you attain in your career will be a function of your

- **Physical well-being**
- **Mental or emotional health**
- **Intellectual strength**

Body, soul, and mind. These three areas will *rely* on good use of your non-working hours. Get good exercise and rest on top of a sensible diet. Find means for personal fulfillment. And stretch your mind through reading and other forms of mental exercise and stimulation. You will see the pay-off.

TIME MANAGEMENT SELF-ANALYSIS
(10 MINUTES)

The following questions are designed to help you determine how strong your Time Management skills are. **Rate each of the questions below according to the following scale:**

0 This is not true for me
1 This is rarely true for me
2 This is seldom true for me
3 This is somewhat true for me
4 This is usually very true for me
5 This is absolutely true for me

**Place an X in the box that best corresponds to you.

		0	1	2	3	4	5
1.	I take time each morning before I start the day to plan each day's activities and consider my priorities.						
2.	I place myself in a situation conducive to creativity every day.						
3.	I am an optimist.						
4.	I spend an average of four hours/week improving my capabilities.						
5.	I do what the boss says to do first.						
6.	It is almost impossible to interrupt me when I am in the middle of focusing on a serious project.						
7.	I control my time all day every day (as opposed to letting circumstances and other people control it).						
8.	I tackle and complete the most important tasks first, and/or during the best part of my working day. (Be honest.)						
9.	I write everything down that I am responsible for remembering to do. (This includes major assignments from the boss, as well as minor types of tasks, such as when a colleague requests a copy of something I have. It also includes personal kinds of things such as getting the dog updated on his vaccines).						
10.	I set deadlines for myself and for the people who report to me.						

(Continued)

		0	1	2	3	4	5
11.	I make minor decisions quickly.						
12.	I delegate jobs to others when practical.						
13.	I make constructive use of my commute time and the time I spend waiting for appointments.						
14.	I write down a set of short-term and long-term goals for my life at least once a year.						
15.	I have the courage to be effective and to say no when appropriate.						
16.	I understand the meaning of "Work smarter, not harder" and how to implement this concept.						
17.	I know the difference between effectiveness and efficiency and, given a choice, which one is more important.						
18.	I approach every major project by establishing goals and setting objectives.						
19.	I take the time to analyze my job and tasks to determine how I can combine things or eliminate things to be more effective.						
20.	I do work that demands more creativity during those times when I will be disturbed the least and when I have the most energy.						
21.	I know my major time-wasters and have some ideas of how to overcome them.						
22.	I handle each piece of paper only once.						

		0	1	2	3	4	5
23.	I communicate clearly. This includes proof-reading everything I send out, including emails. I rehearse oral presentations.						
24.	I do a good job of thinking out issues and questions before presenting them to anybody.						
25.	I take time with my people to train, understand, commit, encourage, appreciate, assist, involve, and promote.						
26.	I know how to plan and conduct, as well as follow up on effective meetings. I always prepare agendas.						
27.	I focus on one task at a time.						
28.	My desk and work area are neat and orderly all day, every day.						
29.	I spend some time in some form of meditation each day.						
30.	I know how to get out of slumps.						
31.	I am familiar with the effects of caffeine and use it to my greatest personal advantage.						
32.	I live a balanced life.						
33.	I get enough rest. (Most people need about eight hours of sleep each night.)						
34.	I do not think about work responsibilities when I am doing non-work kinds of things, such as spending time with my family or playing tennis.						
35.	I enjoy a reasonable amount of leisure or down time for relaxing and doing unimportant things.						

(Continued)

		0	1	2	3	4	5
36.	I am a good family member (e.g., as a wife/husband, mother/father, daughter/son)						
37.	I get enough physical exercise each week. (The CDC says that you need a minimum of 150 minutes of elevated heart rate each week.)						
38.	I eat a balanced diet every day.						
39.	I have a healthy breakfast every morning.						
40.	I am not a Time Management nut.						

Totals						
	x0	x1	x2	x3	x4	x5
equals						

Now total up all the points _____

SCORING: HOW GOOD OF A TIME MANAGER ARE YOU?

200–150 Points: Time Management Expert
149–100 Points: Improvement Warranted
99–50 Points: A Good Start
49–0 Points: You Need Lots of Help!

WEEKLY TIME MANAGEMENT MATRIX

You can use this for planning some structure in your week such as exercise, meditation, and personal development.

	MONDAY	TUESDAY	WEDNESDAY	THURSDAY	FRIDAY	SATURDAY	SUNDAY
6:00–7:00							
7:00–8:00							
8:00–9:00							
9:00–10:00							
10:00–11:00							
11:00–12:00							
12:00–1:00							
1:00–2:00							
2:00–3:00							
3:00–4:00							
4:00–5:00							
5:00–6:00							
6:00–7:00							
7:00–8:00							
8:00–9:00							
9:00–10:00							
10:00–11:00							
11:00–12:00							
12:00–1:00							
1:00–2:00							
2:00–3:00							
3:00–4:00							
4:00–5:00							
5:00–6:00							

Principle

1　2　3　4　5　6　7

Exercise Good Judgment
with Romances

Love can be beautiful. Or it can derail your career. Hormones are powerful! Romantic discretion is an area that is much more challenging and real than many people seem to realize. We tend to treat it privately; which is to say, people do not hear about consequential problems as often as they occur.

Romance in and of itself of course is a wonderful thing! It's just when we make poor decisions that our lives suffer. Infidelity, engaging with someone who is too young, taking an interest in someone where a conflict of interest exists, and other indiscretions normally carry into all other aspects of our lives, including our work (a very BIG component of our lives!), wreaking havoc in ways that we come to greatly regret.

TAKING CARE OF YOUR PERSONAL RELATIONSHIPS

You need to take care of personal relationships in your life. This could include a spouse, children, parents, and/or close friends. Your goal should be to strike an excellent and persistent balance between spending quality time with these people and building your career. If you have a romantic significant other it is particularly important that you and this person work with each other in establishing harmonious personal and professional goals. You need to agree upon how much you want to stress generating more income versus spending more time with each other. The workaholic is criticized in one corner while the lazy is castigated in the other. Different people have different values in this regard. You and your significant other need to be specific about your expectations and desires for each other and seek common ground that you can both be happy with. New romances tend to require much more time initially. In time, the balance can shift mutually. If each person is truly in love, has similar values, is trusting and trustworthy, and is reasonably flexible, you will be able to agree to some parameters.

ROMANCE ISSUES IN THE WORKPLACE

There are two primary concerns in the area of romance voiced by the people I have interviewed over the years:

1. When people develop relationships with other people who work at the same place
2. When people allow romantic problems or issues to carry over into their work

Romances in the Workplace   The Law of Propinquity states that you are more likely to develop a romantic relationship with someone who is physically (i.e., geographically) closer to you. So, people who work in your company are much more likely to become people of romantic interest to you. It just happens. It may not be ideal, but it happens. Maybe in some instances the individuals will decide to stifle it due to professional concerns. Some companies have policies that prohibit it, although not very many. But in cases where the attraction is very strong, employees may be less inclined to worry about professional ramifications.

The *idealists* I have interviewed repeatedly warn against this as career suicide. Some related expressions are, "Don't dip your pen in the company inkwell," "Don't fish off the company pier," and, "Don't swim in the company pool."

The *realists* recognize that it happens and acknowledge that it frequently occurs without any negative impact on the company business. There are even many cases where a person *reports* to their significant other without problems or drawbacks occurring. (Often special arrangements are made in these cases such as having some-one else write the person's annual evaluation.)

There is a book called *Office Mate: The Employee Handbook for Finding—and Managing—Romance on the Job*, by Stephanie Losee and Helaine Olen. They make a case in the book that it is actually smart for today's single co-workers. They suggest that the greatest pool of potential mates is not online or in a bar or on a blind date, but rather in the office. They describe the workplace as the modern-day village or town square, asserting that the office lends itself to old-fashioned courting. They say that more than forty percent of employees at U.S. companies log more than fifty hours a week, so that the people you work with are likely to know you better than your own family. They also point out that for the people to get and keep a job at your company in the first place meant going through considerable filters of integrity.

The obvious biggest drawback to office romances is how they can impact the involved employees and the office environment if the relationship fails. Losee and Olen actually recommend people have a pre-breakup conversation at the beginning of their relationship to try to ameliorate the tensions and conflict that can result from the incident. Losee and Olen emphasize that the most potentially troublesome affairs are between bosses and subordinates, with potential hazards ranging from accusations of favoritism to charges of sexual harassment.

If you do find yourself in a relationship with someone at your worksite, the general advice is to minimize possible concerns as much as you can. Avoid any public displays of affection. Strive to keep your interactive behaviors and public communications as professional and business-focused as possible. Remember that appearance is very important.

When You Bring Romantic Problems to the Workplace   So we're talking here about when people come to work upset over some romantic problem, or when they spend excessive time talking on the phone or texting with their significant other during non-break times. These are distractions that can lead to reduced evaluations and terminations. If you are having problems, just like any other personal problem, these are real and cannot always just be forgotten or ignored during the workday. Just do your best. There is less excuse, however, for excessive communications during the workday, or for taking time off when you shouldn't have. There should be adequate break opportunities to take care of necessary interpersonal communications. Otherwise, delay the romantic exchanges until after work.

LONG-DISTANCE RELATIONSHIPS

You have just accepted a new job that offers great experience, a high salary, and a 500-mile relocation. Now you must figure out how to inform your boyfriend or girlfriend. If you are interested in maintaining the relationship, the announcement itself will probably be the least of your problems.

Over one million couples are living in separate U.S. cities today, and another 700,000 long-distance relationship (LDR) couples are actually married. It is a myth that most fail (Amatenstein, 2006). However, anybody who has engaged in such a relationship will tell you that LDRs are very different and very challenging.

Individuals in LDRs seem to worry much more about affairs than those in geographically close relationships. As one person said to me, "The biggest problem is when she calls and hears other people, especially girls, in the background. She gets jealous and I have to spend time assuring her that nothing is going on." When one is involved in an LDR, it is important to remain optimistic about the relationship. Don't worry about things you cannot control. Misunderstandings increase because of the lack of face-to-face contact. Facial expressions, hand gestures, and other forms of body language are important communication tools. You often have to give this up in an LDR.

Make time to do things that draw the two of you closer. Engage in multiple forms of communication. Today's technology, such as texting, email, webcams, and cell phones make LDRs much easier. Written communication is often more effective in communicating true feelings than the telephone.

Whether you live apart or together, it is also important not to make your partner your whole life. You should get involved in other organizations and activities. The aim is "compromise, not sacrifice." Do not isolate yourself. You can still be a social person (Ibid).

Younger couples who enter into long-distance relationships usually make one of three types of arrangements that I will label:

The Break-Up ♦ Semi-Committed ♦ All the Way

The balance of this chapter will discuss each of these ideas, suggesting some pros and cons and concluding with a personal recommendation. There is obviously no simple solution.

The Break-Up

The Break-up option severs the relationship right up front, with the two individuals proceeding on their own ways. Few people seem to choose the Break-up option (initially). This may be the most difficult of the three options. The main advantage in this decision is that the couple does not experience the tensions of trying to sustain a long-distance relationship. Another advantage may be that the pain, frustration, and misery can be much shorter than that of the other options.

The disadvantage to breaking up is obvious: You're in love! Why ruin a good thing?! Good matches are difficult to come by. Developing the relationship can take even more time. Thus, it might not make sense to give up a mutually satisfying relationship for the benefit of avoiding a stressful period of time.

Semi-Committed

The Semi-Committed option appears to be the most popular alternative. The ground rules go something like this:

"We will still consider ourselves together."
"We may both go out with other people just for fun."
"We will stop going out with other people once we are both back in the same area."

This option is an obvious attempt to "have your cake and eat it too"; where couples want to have the best of both worlds. The advantage of this option is that it allows you to maintain the relationship and yet still enjoy the companionship of others in activities like movies and dancing.

The problems that result from a semi-committed relationship can often be devastating. As it turns out, individuals usually experience a great deal of jealousy. Though they like the idea of dating other people, they cannot stand the idea of the other person being with someone else. The problem often becomes more ridiculous and complicated as the individuals become jealous of another person, and at the same time are themselves developing stronger feelings for someone else in their own vicinity. What irony! As one person said to me: "I find myself constantly being attracted to the girls around me here. Yet every time my girlfriend does something with another guy, I get all upset and jealous."

The truth is, many people fall into the trap believing that not only can they allow their partner to date without it bothering them, but that it's also easy for them to date other people in a casual, uncommitted way without developing any romantic feelings toward them.

All the Way

The final option is the All-the-Way plan, sometimes coined as Do or Die or Till Death Do Us Part. Both members of the couple feel that their relationship is worth maintaining at all costs, and they therefore make a commitment to be completely true to each other and to not date anybody else ... ever!

There are several advantages to this plan. The key advantage is that a joint commitment by the couple increases the chances of the relationship surviving. Also, the couple will most likely experience less jealousy-related tension and stress. Finally, with dating activities removed from the week, the individuals have more time to work and accomplish other goals.

There are also several disadvantages. Loneliness and boredom can set in. And many long-distance relationships result in one or both individuals idealizing each other through the long periods of absence. They imagine the other to be more than they really are. (One reason absence sometimes seems to make the heart grow fonder?) Then when the couple reunites, the disillusionment can test the relationship.

If you don't believe in the impact of these illusions, consider this: How many times have you had an interest in someone, only to quickly lose interest after you finally went out once with them? Part of the explanation for this common phenomenon is that people develop less-than-accurate images of other people. These images are corrected after first-hand experience with the other person.

Which Plan is for You?

Any recommendations as to which plan you should follow would naturally vary with different individuals, cultures, and circumstances. It might make a difference, for example, if you were going to be 100 miles apart for three weeks or 2,000 miles apart for two years.

The starting point of course is to discuss it with each other. You should specifically discuss the following questions:

1. How strong are your feelings for each other?
2. How far has your relationship developed?
3. What kind of potential does your relationship have?
4. What kind of a commitment are you willing to make to each other?

This discussion can serve as an objective basis for your decision, provided that you are honest and open with each other. Good communication is critical.

Your next step is to decide which plan you want to go with. I would submit that the Semi-Committed plan proves to be the most difficult. I have seen too many cases where a couple tried this and at least one of the members experienced serious depression and anxiety. The Semi-Committed plan is usually a drawn-out (de facto) version of the Break-up plan. It just doesn't ever seem to work.

Long-distance relationships are difficult and confusing. Have a brutally frank talk with your partner about how serious you are and what your expectations and levels of commitment really are. If you decide to try it, strive for tons of communication during the time apart. And if possible, set a limit on how long you plan to be apart.

The Test?!

It seems that in nearly every discussion regarding long-distance relationships, somebody makes the suggestion that the distance serves as a valuable test. That is, if the relationship were really meant to be, it would last. A popular poster promotes this idea reading something like: "If you love something, let it go. If it comes back to you, then it is yours. If not, then it never was."

Certainly marriages must endure endless difficulties and challenges. This may offer some merit to the idea of a long-distance relationship being a valuable test. However, to say that the relationship was not meant to be is a hasty oversimplification, failing to recognize the need to approach each test with care, diligence, and intelligent strategies.

Close Opposite-Sex Friends

How many times have you heard: "My best friends have always been of the opposite sex" or "I have always felt more comfortable talking with people of the opposite sex"? Close relationships often *lead to* romance. As one contemporary philosopher quipped, "Man is not a rational animal, (Rousseau) he is a rationalizing animal" (Heinlein 1953). Don't kid yourself. If you want to maintain a long-distance relationship, your safest course of action is to develop close friendships people you are not likely to develop romantic feelings for.

We Were Made for Each Other

Another common misconception is the idea that two people are made for each other. Social science studies do not bear this out. There are any number of people out there who can make for a good match with a given individual.

Final Suggestions

If you do decide to break off or suspend your relationship, you can always do it with the mutual understanding that if and when you come back into closer proximity to each other, you could always get back together at that time if both of you are still eligible.

If on the other hand you decide to maintain your relationship ALL THE WAY, prepare to give 110%. It is imperative that BOTH members be 110% interested and committed to making the relationship work. Consider the following ground rules in making your long-distance relationship thrive (especially relevant to those on smaller budgets):

- No dating. Avoid any situations where you might find yourself alone with someone of the opposite sex. Think twice before you do *anything* with the opposite sex. You certainly should not do anything with another person that you would not do if your partner were there to see it.
- Communicate with each other every day at least once. If you were not apart, you would most likely spend at least an hour a day talking to each other in person. So taking a few minutes here and there throughout the day to communicate should be easy.
- People often feel that they have to make many lengthy phone calls when they are feeling insecure about their relationship. They want or "need" to hear in their partner's voice that they still love them. A couple should take care to avoid the habit where one member says, "I love you" just to get the same response from the other member. There are better ways to deal with such anxiety such as talking directly about it in person whenever there is an opportunity to get together.
  - By the way, feeling insecure is a legitimate, natural, and common feeling. It does not mean that one member in the relationship is in any way weaker than the other.
  - Nonetheless, work on your self-security and feelings of independence if this is a problem.
- Set some new and personal goals for yourselves. It will help the time to pass more quickly. Again, take advantage of your new spare time. (See Principle #6 for additional ideas.)
- Continue to enjoy life. Enjoy yourself. Enjoy your partner as much as you can. Make the best of your situation. Think positively.

- Keep yourself busy. People seem to suffer loneliness and jealousy the most during their idle time.
- Work on your trust levels; that is, work on trusting your partner. Work at making yourself trustworthy. "Trust" is an easy idea to define, but difficult to put into real practice.

Appendix A

Basic IRS Taxation Definitions and Model

This appendix provides a little bit more depth on how income taxation works in the U.S. As was mentioned earlier, I recommend you do further reading throughout the rest of your life on personal tax laws and investment strategies. They are constantly changing. I also recommend you hire a certified public accountant (CPA) to prepare your tax returns for you each year. Like many things (such as building a fence), you can figure out how to do them yourself, but it will take some time, and the chances of your getting them exactly right the first time are slim. The cost of hiring a CPA is not that high, and the resulting peace of mind is well worth the cost in my opinion. There are many books published each year to help taxpayers figure out what the tax laws are supposed to mean and what is permissible. The CPAs do this research each year to the benefit of all their clients.

The following provides good *basic* information that will help you to work with your CPA more intelligently and effectively.

Gross Income: Your total income and earnings during a calendar or fiscal year. There are very few sources of income that are not considered taxable according to the IRS. IRA interest, interest on U.S. Savings Bonds, and tax-exempt municipal bonds are few of the exceptions. (Note, however, that income tax is merely deferred on all earnings on traditional IRAs and saving bonds. With the IRS, it's usually either now or later.)

Adjusted Gross Income (AGI): Your gross income less certain costs such as IRAs and pension contributions (collectively referred to as Deductions from Gross Income).

Standard vs. Itemized Tax Deductions: The government has specified certain types of personal expenditures as legitimate tax deductions (or write-offs) that may be subtracted from your adjusted gross income before you compute the amount of income tax that you will owe. The IRS allows you to either take a standard, non-itemized deduction or to fill out a detailed itemized analysis to calculate an itemized deduction (Schedule A).

You can figure out your total itemized deductions to see which one will net you the greatest deduction. (In other words, unless your fully itemized Schedule A deductions are greater than the standard deduction allowed by the IRS, the itemized deductions won't do you any good.)

Some examples of typical allowed deductions:

- Un-reimbursed employee business expenses (that are more than 2% of AGI)
- Charitable contributions
- Interest payments toward a home loan
- Property taxes
- Medical and dental bills, including prescriptions and the mileage to go to the doctor and return, (the total of all medical bills must exceed 7½% of your AGI)

- Union dues
- Required uniforms or protective coverings
- Portions of your auto license fee
- State and local income taxes paid

Personal Exemption: The IRS gives every taxpayer at least one personal deduction (to be subtracted from AGI) of $6,100 (2013). A deduction of the same amount may be subtracted from AGI for your spouse, each additional child, and even a parent or relative who is living with you as long as these dependents fall within IRS guidelines. Likewise, note that you cannot claim a personal exemption if your parents have claimed you as an exemption for the same tax year.

Taxable Income: The total AGI minus your standard or itemized deductions, and minus your personal exemption(s). Your tax rate is based on the amount of your taxable income.

Summary

Gross Income
—Deductions from Gross Income (e.g., IRA)
Adjusted Gross Income

Adjusted Gross Income
—Standard or Itemized Deductions
—Personal Exemption (s)
Taxable Income

Example:

Suppose that you earned $25,000.00 during the first year of your job. During the twelve months of the year that you worked (from January 1 to December 31), you had the following expenses that qualify as legitimate deductions (remember that you must have receipts, credit card statements, or canceled checks available to substantiate each expense):

Church contributions:	$3,000.00
Non-Reimbursed Business Expenses:	
(before 2% limit):	$1,470.00
Total Itemized Deductions:	**$4,470.00**

Suppose during the year you started an IRA and paid into it $1,500.00.

Here's what your IRS tax liability might look like when you file your return for the year:

Gross Income	$25,000.00
Less IRA Deduction	− $1,500.00
Total Adjusted Gross Income:	$23,500.00
Less the IRS Standard Deduction (If you decide not to itemize):	− $6,100.00
OR	
The sum of your itemized deductions:	− $4,470.00

(Note that it would be advisable this tax year to not itemize your deductions because they are less than your Standard Deduction of $6,100.00.)

Less Your **Itemized Deduction**	− $6,100.00
Less Your **Personal Exemption**	− $3,300.00
Taxable Income	$14,100.00

Suppose the tax rate on $14,100 is 15%.

Then the IRS Tax Owed = 15% × $14,100 = $2,115.

If you had claimed one exemption on your W-4 when you started your job, your employer probably already deducted about $3,000.00 from your paychecks for federal withholding, affording you a refund of $885.

Many people prefer to have a little extra taken out of their paychecks each month as a forced savings method. The most prudent financial managers, however, have as little money taken out as possible, allowing themselves to invest that much more of their earnings, rather than have it sitting idle in the government coffers.

Tax-Rate Variance

The higher your taxable income, the higher your tax rate. However, as you graduate into higher tax brackets, it is only the taxable income above the previous tax bracket that is taxed at that new, higher rate. For example, suppose the tax rate for earnings up to $15,000 were ten percent, and that the tax rate from $15,000 to $30,000 were 15 percent. What would your tax rate be if you make $20,000?

The misperception is that you would have to pay: $20,000 × 15 percent = $3,000

The correct answer:

[$15,000 × 10 percent] + [(the remaining) $5,000 × 15 percent] = $2,250.

Appendix B

Dining Etiquette

Manners are important. Executives consider social skills as important as other business skills. You can see a clear correlation between employment level and manners; maybe ten percent of entry-level professionals have impeccable manners, fifty percent of mid-management personnel, and ninety-nine percent of CEOs.

New professionals are often uneasy about their dining etiquette. Familiarity with the following rules may build your self-confidence.

1. Keep your cell phone off.
2. Place your napkin on your lap as soon as you and your party are seated. When you leave the table temporarily, put it on your seat. When you are finished eating, place the napkin to the left of your plate. Never shake it out or use it as a bib.
3. Don't talk about the features of the formal table setting. This just tells your party that you were raised without such enculturation.
4. Treat the restaurant staff with your best cordialness.

5. Avoid being the only person drinking alcohol. And never feel like you *need* to drink. And if you don't drink in general, you do not need to explain yourself. If you *do* drink, know your limits and never exceed them.

6. Refrain from picking up your menu until your host has picked up his or hers.

7. If it is a business meal, refrain from discussing any business until everybody has ordered. And try to not pass around any documents until everybody has finished eating.

8. Hold your wine glass by putting your first two fingers and thumb at the bottom of the bowl with your last two fingers touching the stem.

9. Women should blot their lipstick on a tissue. Avoid leaving a lipstick smudge on your glass or napkin.

10. If you need to take medicine or freshen up your cosmetics, do this in the restroom.

11. Your bread plate goes on the left and your water glass is on the right. Remember the rule this way: Food has four letters and so does the word "left"; drink has five letters and so does the word "right." Another way to remember is to raise both hands, and put your index fingers to your thumbs. You will see that your left hand forms a "b" for bread, and your right hand forms a "d" for drink.

12. Don't take someone else's bread or drink from another person's glass.

13. Do not hold up the order because you can't decide what you want to eat. Also, be judicious in how many items you ask the server to explain. Otherwise you will annoy people with your indecisiveness.

14. Order meals that are less messy and difficult. Consider the "splash" potential. Foods like hamburgers or chicken that beg for personal contact with your fingers should be avoided. Spaghetti and other pastas can be difficult AND messy. If you don't know how to eat it, don't order it.

15. If this is a business luncheon or dinner, follow your host's lead. If he or she orders wine, then it is okay for you to. Likewise, if he or she orders something extravagant, or if he or she orders dessert, then it is okay for you to.

16. Don't double dip (e.g., don't dig a carrot into a dip after you have taken a bite of the carrot).

17. Invite other people to help themselves and serve themselves first.

18. Don't use your own utensils to serve yourself from a serving dish. Ask for a serving fork or spoon.

19. If you have multiple utensils by your plate, you will use the outermost first, and work your way in.

20. Remember that the smaller fork is always used for salads or appetizers.

21. Don't use a pitchfork hold or a cello grip on your eating utensils. It looks uncouth to hold your fork like it's a toothbrush.

22. Lean forward and meet your fork with your mouth when eating a salad. If a piece of lettuce falls, it will land on your plate and not on the front of your shirt, blouse, or lap.

23. Once you have begun using your utensils, rest them on the edge of your plate when not using them. Don't set them back on the table. Rest the knife on the back edge.

24. Don't break crackers into your soup.

25. Use a serving spoon to bring some jam or jelly to your plate from the jar or container that they are served in. Then use your butter knife to spread the jelly on your roll. Do not stick your own knife or spoon into the containers.

26. Don't mash or stir your food.

27. Don't speak with your mouth full. Chew with your mouth closed.

28. Try to eat at the same pace as others at the table.

29. Keep your elbows off the table until you are finished eating.

30. Use your napkin to wipe your mouth and fingers once in a while. Never lick your fingers.

31. Don't lick your utensils either.
32. Keep your elbows down low but comfortable. Pretend you have a book tucked up high under each arm.
33. Don't wave your fork or knife around in the air while speaking.
34. Don't pick up crumbs that fall or spill onto the table. Leave them there. If you drop pieces of food, you can pick them up with your utensils and leave them on the side of the plate. Don't worry about food that falls on the floor. If you think it is necessary, you can alert your server to it.
35. When you have lulls in the conversation, take a drink of your water. This keeps you from feeling dumb while you and your party think of something else to say.
36. Speak in a well-modulated voice at the table. Avoid subjects that might make guests uncomfortable.
37. Cover your nose and mouth with your sleeve and turn your head when you have to sneeze.
38. Don't use a toothpick or dental floss in public.
39. Don't eat your ice cubes.
40. When you are finished eating, you can leave your utensils resting together on your plate with the tips in the middle of the plate. This signals to your server that you are finished.
41. Do not fight over the check. If the host, or the person who invited you, offers to pay for you, you can offer one time to pay for your share or the tip. If they still want to pay for it, you should allow them to, regardless of gender.

Worrying about these rules can at first take the fun out of eating out. But one of the signs of a professional is the ability to demonstrate excellent poise and posture in every situation. Eating is one of those areas of grace and poise at which you can either come out looking like Emily Post or Mister Ed.

Appendix C

Business-World Jargon and Expressions

T he following phrases are commonly encountered by new professionals as:

Brand new to you
Not fully understood by you,
Or, unfamiliar in their origin to you.

To enhance your comprehension and command of workplace communication, skim the following phrases, focusing in on those of interest.

A

To arch your back: Prepare to fight, as a cat arches its back in anticipation of a fight.

It'll cost you an arm and a leg: In George Washington's days, there were no cameras. One's image was either sculpted or painted. Some paintings of George Washington showed him standing behind a desk with one arm behind his back while others showed both legs and both arms. Prices charged by painters were not based on how many people were to be painted, but by how many limbs were to be painted. Hence the statement "Okay, but it'll cost you an arm and a leg."

Keep at an arm's length away: Implies that you are getting closer to someone, but that you are not ready to trust them completely yet.

(Break your arm) patting yourself on the back: Self-congratulatory. Excessively proud of yourself.

B

Throw the baby out with the bath water: Remove ALL of something (e.g., a staff or a program) with the intent of getting rid of something bad, but in the process losing something else that was very valuable (if not the most important component).

To show some backbone or spine: Daring; courageous.

Bailiwick: One's jurisdiction; area of responsibility or expertise.

Get the ball rolling: To overcome the initial inertia of getting something going or in progress.

Whole ball of wax: Indicates entirety. Popular phrase on Madison Avenue in 1960s. May be in reference to Madame Tussaud's wax works.

Banana Republic: Lit: A small country that is economically dependent on a single export commodity, such as bananas. Implies that a department or company relies on one single product or service.

Cover all of your bases: Prepare for all possible occurrences or situations.

To be given a cold bath: To startle, such as with surprising news; perhaps implying the person should have known the information already. Like a wake-up call or rude awakening.

Win the battle and lose the war: The idea of winning something in the short run, such as an argument, that ends up causing you to lose much more in the long run. For example, you prove somebody wrong in an argument, so they end up demoting you out of spite later on.

Pick your battles: Presumes there are many issues with many people that you could take on. So you should decide which ones are most important to you, and let the others go.

Get in bed with (bed partners or bedfellows): To get in close with another person or group; close associate or ally.

You made your bed, now lie in it: Endure the consequences of your own mistakes.

Bedrock: Basis or foundation. Orig.: The solid rock underlying soil.

Benchmark: A standard by which something can be measured or judged.

To be sold a bill of goods: An investment that ends up being worthless. May connote malicious intent of seller.

To bird-dog: To watch closely and possibly seek out (as does a bird dog). To steal another's date (e.g., at a party).

Blink first: To give in or make the first careless error.

To sweat blood: To work real hard, perhaps implying nervousness.

Changing boats (or horses) in the middle of the stream (or race): To change ideas or goals as a project is being completed.

To throw (the dog) a bone: To do something for someone that might cause them to suddenly begin to like you and want to support you.

Boom or bust: To do either very well or very poorly, especially financially.

Bread-and-butter product: The basic, low-risk product that a company relies on to stay in business. The money-making solid base.

In the same breath: Sense of urgency in offering a second, related remark. For example, "And in the same breath I would say ... "

Brick and mortar: The very basic components, resources, or building blocks necessary for the development of something.

Cross that bridge when we come to it: To deal with a problem when you really need to, rather than worry about it prematurely.

Browbeat: To intimidate with an overbearing manner; bully.

Take the bull by the horns: To deal with a problem, concern, or situation directly and squarely.

To sweat bullets: Extreme nervousness.

To burn the midnight oil: To work hard, long, and especially late (burning lantern oil during the night to provide light to work by).

To burn one's bridges: To destroy a person's beneficiary relationship with a person, group, or service (e.g., through personal insults).

Put on the back burner: To put something worthwhile aside temporarily until it is needed or you are ready for it. To let it simmer passively while you are tending to other matters.

C

To have your cake and eat it too: To want two things that are mutually exclusive. For example, "We need to get our employees to work long hours and persuade them at the same time that we want them to live balanced lives." (It would be more obvious if it went, "To save your cake and eat it too.")

To call on or be put on the carpet: Reprimand, scold, or tell off. Implies that the receiver of a reprimand responds sheepishly with their head down.

To open a can of worms: To bring up a subject that upsets others present and suddenly has to be dealt with. Complex situation.

Canary in a (coal) mine: Life for an actual canary in a coal mine could be described in three words: short but meaningful. Early coal mines did not feature ventilation systems, so miners would routinely bring a caged canary into new coal seams. Canaries are especially sensitive to methane and carbon monoxide, which made them ideal for detecting any dangerous gas build-ups. As long as the canary in a coal mine kept singing, the miners knew their air supply was safe. A dead canary in a coal mine signaled an immediate evacuation. (http://www.wisegeek.com/what-does-it-mean-to-be-a-canary-in-a-coal-mine.htm)

Like using a cannon when a flyswatter will do: Overkill. An excessive response.

In the cards: Fate. Prediction or prophecy based on instinct; gut feeling that is probably based on other less-than-obvious evidences. (Orig.: Fortune-telling based on cards.)

Lay your cards on the table: Be upfront; aggressively open; honest.

Play cards close to the vest: Secretive.

Put the cart before the horse: To do or say something in a backward order.

Carve up the pie: Refers to dividing up something (usually something good) such as budgetary funds.

Cast in concrete (stone): Irreversible decision or action.

Catch 22: There is no solution; only circular attempts. Orig.: Underlying theme in the book *Catch 22*. You can get out of the army if you are insane, but you must apply to get out. If you are able to apply to get out of the army, you must not be insane.

Like herding cats: Virtually impossible.

Sort out the chaff: To filter out the bad part (just as a combine removes the chaff of the wheat stalk.)

Beat your chest (on how great you are): Unwarranted bragging. Overconfidence.

Like a bull in a china shop: Recklessness in a particularly fragile or sensitive situation.

Take to the cleaners: Cheat or rip off to great excess, especially financially.

Test the climate (or air, or water): Check status, attitude, or latest beliefs of a group of people or a situation.

Dark cloud on the horizon: Something negative anticipated.

Having your head in the clouds: Being unrealistic about a situation.

To turn the corner: To get to a point when you see major progress; nearly finished; seeing light at the end of the tunnel.

The first crack in the dam: Indication of a major problem potentially getting ready to occur.

Cream always rises to the top: To suggest that the best is always recognized eventually.

A crock: Something fallacious, pretentious, or unwise. Negative connotation. Refers to "crock of feces." Before indoor toilets, in winter, people had a large ceramic crock as a toilet, so as not to have to go outside.

Caught in the crossfire: To be in between somebody else's fighting/debating.

Bet on the come: To make decisions or take actions where you are assuming with extreme confidence that something else will be delivered as promised.

Cupbearer: Person who tests something out before anybody else. Orig.: 1. A person who served someone like a king by eating or drinking a sample of what was to be served to them to make sure it was safe and free of any poisons. 2. A person who delivers the cup; in this case news, or information. News can be good or bad, but normally this is used in reference to bad news. Orig.: Refers to the person who carried the cup of poison to the condemned; in particular Socrates.

Cutting Edge: As advanced as possible.

D

DTS: "Decline to state," as in response to a survey question.

Water over the dam: A mistake was made, but it is too late to go back and change it now. Just move on without dwelling on the mistake.

Carry the day: Win, prevail, as in, "At auctions the wealthiest bidders usually carry the day."

Dead man walking: Orig.: A person on death row who is walking to his or her execution. Refers to someone whom everyone presumes is going to be fired.

Playing with a full deck: At one time in history there was a tax levied when purchasing playing cards, but only applicable to the ace of spades. To avoid paying the tax, people would purchase 51 cards instead. Yet, since most games require 52 cards, these people were thought to be stupid or dumb because they weren't playing with a full deck.

To take a deep six: Go under, be destroyed, fall through.

Get off the dime: To do something; initiative.

In dire straits: In severe difficulty or trouble.

Dog paddle: To struggle for sustenance or maintenance. To fight to keep your head above water.

Bet your bottom dollar: Absolute certainty.

Drag your feet: To be reluctant. Move slowly, perhaps in caution or not being sure of yourself.

Beat that drum: As in "I have beat that drum for several years," meaning that you have been pushing or promoting that idea for so long.

Wait for the dust to settle: To wait in determining or assessing a total situation after a major event has occurred that had potentially wide-ranging repercussions. This allows time to ascertain what other related ramifications or responses might have come from the occurrence.

E

Have your ear to the ground: To watch or pay careful attention to an event. (Just as you can hear something like a train coming from a distance by putting your ear to the ground.)

To eighty-six it: To cancel or do away with something (e.g., an idea or plan).

Push the envelope: Strive for more and more improvement. For example, Faster computer, stronger material, etc.

Back-of-an-envelope: Done quickly and lacking thoroughness, as in a back-of-an-envelope calculation.

On an even keel: To be balanced. To get along; compatibility. An even keel on a boat keeps it balanced.

An exercise in futility: A hopeless task or waste of time.

F

Face the music: To face or accept and deal with a given situation or predicament.

Losing face: Suffer embarrassment or humility. In older days, personal hygiene left much room for improvement. As a result, many women and men had developed acne scars by adulthood. The women would spread bee's wax over their facial skin to smooth out their complexions. When they were speaking to each other, if a woman began to stare at another woman's face she was told "mind your own bee's wax." Should the woman smile, the wax would crack, hence the term "crack a smile." Also, when they sat too close to the fire, the wax would melt, which brought about the statement "losing face."

The fair-haired boy: A manager's pet who seems to receive favored treatment.

As easy as falling off a log: Extremely easy.

Feast or famine: Boom or bust. Things either go great or horribly. There's no in-between. One day you have more business than you can handle, then maybe a few months later, you do not have nearly enough.

Feather your own nest: To do something for yourself; to protect your own turf; to improve your situation, perhaps subtly.

Get your feet wet: To lightly or briefly experience something before greater immersion. To start something.

Riding the fence: Describes a person who will not commit to one side or the other, such as on an issue.

Play second fiddle: To be the second person in the line of authority or responsibility, especially in reference to who gets the credit or who is in the limelight. Orig.: The best violinist in a symphony, who normally gets most of the leads or solos, is entitled the first violinist.

FIFO: First in, first out. (See "Sausage.")

Go over with a fine-tooth comb: To review or search through very carefully and thoroughly.

Fine tune: To put the finishing touches on something; to polish or shine it up.

To have your fingerprints on something: To have had a part in doing or creating something.

Put out fires: To take care of little problems that suddenly arise rather than dealing with planned progressive work.

Neither fish nor fowl: Something in between, or a little of both.

Fish or cut bait: A command to be decisive. Either do it or don't. Opposite of indecision.

Bare-fisted or bare-knuckled: Suggests bluntness or dirtiness in a fight or debate.

Flex your muscles: To demonstrate or show off strength or abilities through a relatively minor exhibition.

Fly-by-night: Implies instability. Refers to a person or operation that all of a sudden comes onto the scene to take advantage of people by selling something, and then quickly leaves. Orig.: Occasionally peddlers would come into town one day, sell their products, and sneak out of town that night before the townspeople discovered the product was no good.

Get your foot in the door: To begin to establish yourself, usually toward obtaining a certain position. A person wanting to get his or her foot in the door of a company for long-term employment might begin by accepting a part-time or temporary position with them.

To follow in the footsteps of: To be compared to one's predecessor.

Can't see the forest for the trees: Having such a vested interest in something that you are unable to see or recognize the entire picture, but rather only individual parts.

Paper foxhole: Place of hiding or protection, especially in terms of legalities.

Freeload: To live off another person or take advantage of them without offering to pay.

To be on the front line: To go to where the action or work is actually taking place, the site of execution. Negative connotation if a person has never been in the trenches. (Orig.: Refers to soldiers in the trenches of the war frontlines.)

To fuel the fire: To make people angrier or make matters worse through additional remarks or actions.

To lay the groundwork for: To do good preliminary work for a future endeavor.

G

Run the gauntlet: To endeavor a difficult undertaking. Orig.: Tribal practice of running between two lines of people beating you with sticks.

Glitch: Something wrong in the system. A termed popularized in computer programming.

Don't let grass grow under your feet: Keep busy or active, especially after an event that is typically stifling or shocking. Do not stand around.

As interesting or exciting as watching grass grow (or paint dry): Dull. Slow moving.

Gilding the lily: To try to improve something that is already perfect.

To move the goal posts: Increasing or changing minimum expectations given to someone.

H

Half-cocked: Tensely ready to explode in anger, as a gun that is half-cocked is ready to go off.

Hamstrung: To disable or handicap. Orig.: By cutting tendons in the leg.

The right hand doesn't know what the left hand is doing: Suggests poor communication within an organization. (The two halves of the brain are connected by a few single nerve cords. If you sever these cords, the left side of the body does not know what the right side is doing.)

School of hard knocks: To learn by experience and mistakes.

Beat your head against the wall: Implies working hard on something, but in vain.

Trading a headache for a stomachache: An action that eliminates one problem, only to result in a new problem (of comparable significance).

Nipping at your heels: Annoying you toward a certain position, or away from another, as a dog might nip at a cow's heels.

To hedge: To protect oneself, especially financially (e.g., hedging one's bet).

Hem and Haw: Suggests a person is not directly and outwardly responding or saying what he or she has to say, perhaps because they are caught by surprise, embarrassed over the matter, etc.

Ride herd on: To supervise closely; to put continual pressure on someone to accomplish a task. Orig.: Cattlemen ride herd on cattle, continually forcing them to move forward without straying.

Keep a person in your hip pocket: To keep a person interested in you and in your favor. To have enough favors owed to you so the other person will do almost anything for you.

Tough row to hoe: Difficult job or task ahead.

You get more with honey than vinegar: Positive incentives motivate personnel production better than threats.

Honeymoon period: Period of increased tolerance or favor by supervisors and peers during initial period of employment or association.

By hook or by crook: By whatever means possible, fair or unfair. [Shepherds used the hook of their staff to pull a sheep, or the crook (i.e., the other end) of their staff to prod them.]

Hornet's nest: A precariously upset place or situation.

Beat a dead horse: To criticize something that cannot be fixed or is no longer an issue for some reason. Or, to go on and on about a matter that has already been discussed sufficiently.

To have one's house in order: Well organized and prepared.

I

Trading insults: Someone says something derogatory to one person, so the other person just responds with something derogatory about them, with this continuing pointlessly.

To run interference: To meet and take care of or block any opposition or problems (as a blocker does for a runner in football) for an upcoming person or event.

Return on your investment: (ROI) Employees are an expensive investment and if they do not do enough for the company, the company has no return on their investment in them, possibly resulting in termination.

Too many irons in the fire: Too many commitments or responsibilities.

J

JIT Method: Just-in-Time method used in ordering parts or supplies to arrive only when the company is ready to use them, rather than stockpiling.

Jury-rig (or Jerry-rig): Construct in a makeshift fashion.

K

Rap over the knuckles: To chide or reprimand.

L

Lambaste: To tell someone off (making someone feel like he or she has been lambasted).

Lame duck: Person who lacks clout because they are soon to leave their position or office of authority. Also used to refer to presidents in their second four-year term to mean they do not have to please the voters with what is being done.

Lead pipe cinch: A sure thing. Arranged or set with virtually 100% certainty.

Leading edge/bleeding edge: As advanced as possible.

Sponge or leech: See "Freeload."

Left-handed compliment: A compliment in an awkward or round-about way.

To go out on a limb: To take a chance, as in climbing to the end of a tree branch and hoping it holds your weight.

Toe the line: Abide by the rules.

The lion's share: The largest portion.

At loggerheads with each other: To work out of harmony, in disagreement, or in contention against another person. Often the two are supposed to be supporting each other (e.g., working for the same firm).

A lock: A sure thing. Arranged or set with virtually 100% certainty.

To have a long memory: Seems to remember longer than normal those things that people do or say, perhaps especially for the purpose of using them against the people.

Looking at the world through rose-colored glasses: To be optimistic to the point of not seeing anything negative around you.

No love lost: Refers to negative feelings between two people who are ending an association of some sort.

The lowdown: The inside facts. The whole story.

There ain't no such thing as a free lunch: The idea that nothing is ever really free, even if announced as such. For example, a gift from a colleague or contractor often means they plan to ask for a favor of reciprocation sometime down the road, if not immediately. Sometimes abbreviated TANSTAAFL and pronounced Tan-sta-fle.

M

MBWA: Management by Wandering Around. Common saying in Fortune 500 companies encouraging managers to get out among their employees more.

Melting pot: Place, organization, or situation in which many types and/or races of people or ideas mix and interact. Implies assimilation.

Middle-of-the-road: Describes a person who will not commit to one side or the other, such as on an issue.

Milestone: A significant point in development. Orig.: a stone serving as a milepost.

Still has milk on his lips (green; wet behind the ears): Young; novice; newly matured; inexperienced.

Like running in molasses: A struggle. Slow.

Monkey on your back: A burden; an inanimate object looking over your shoulder to keep you in line. Orig.: A heroin addict is said to have a monkey on his back (something you cannot get rid of and that you have to continually feed heroin).

Clear as mud: Ambiguous.

Music to my ears: Good news.

N

Nature of the beast: A trait or characteristic inherent in something.

Nemesis: An enemy or rival. Someone who bugs you to do something. Orig.: The Greek goddess of retributive justice.

Nuts and bolts: Common or mundane part of a system. For example, "He has a nuts and bolts approach—he takes the tried and true approach, not new or imaginative."

In a nutshell: To encapsulate into a small amount or an abbreviated picture.

O

Put one's oar in the water: To initiate personal involvement in an attempt to influence, steer, or assist in a given situation.

Off-line: At another time or outside of the meeting, as in, "We can discuss it further off-line," or some other day.

Outgrowth: Something developing or springing forth by surprise from some other process or activity.

Old hat: Well-known or old information.

OEM: Original Equipment Manufacturer.

P

To mind your p's and q's: The saying generally advises people to be prudent. According to Brewer's Dictionary of Phrase and Fable, the phrase may be derived from an admonition to children learning the alphabet to be careful distinguishing between the letters "p" and "q," or to printers' apprentices in handling and sorting type. It may have also been used as a caution to tavern customers to mind their p's and q's while paying their tabs. They ordered beer by p's for pints and q's for quarts.

Pan out: Successful effort or attempt. Orig.: panning for gold.

To open Pandora's box: To do something that brings about adverse ramifications or reactions and cannot be reversed. Orig.: Greek mythology.

Up to par: Usual or normal value or performance. Orig.: Face value of a bond.

Fit a square peg in a round hole: Poor fit, combination, or match.

To give (one) pause: A thought or action that causes a person to stop and think. Cause one to hesitate.

Penny-wise, pound-foolish: To worry about short-term gains at the loss of much greater long-term gains.

Peter Principle: The idea that all professionals advance to a position or level one step above that which they are capable of handling well. Orig.: Peter Drucker published the idea.

Photo finish: The finish of a race that is so close that a picture is necessary for determination of a winner (horse racing).

Pick-and-shovel work: Implies slow, more time-consuming, and maybe lower-level work.

Pig in a poke: Something unknown that proves to be inferior or flawed, as buying a product from a supplier you are unfamiliar with, only to discover it was no good. ("Poke" is a word meaning "brown paper bag" used in Appalachia.) Common expression is "Don't buy a pig in a poke."

Pigeon-holed: To assign to a single category or task. May imply over-restrictiveness. To put in an out-of-the-way place so as not to worry about it now, but so it is available at a later date.

Piggyback on an idea: To build upon an already presented idea.

Get your pink slip: Find out you are being laid off, released, or fired. This is how some companies notify their employees of this action.

Cross-pollinated: To get input from multiple sources.

Pollyanna: Taken from the movie with the same name, referring to a person who is so nice that they appear surreal.

To test the pulse: To analyze or assess a group's feelings, thoughts, attitudes (as the blood pulse is a health indicator).

If push comes to shove: If all else fails. If worse comes to worst. If it turns out that all other alternatives have been tried.

Pot calling the kettle black: To accuse someone of something or to describe derogatorily as something that is also true of you. (Might sound racist. I recommend you not use this one.)

Preaching to the choir: Presenting a case for something to somebody who already subscribes to what you are saying.

Pull punches: To hold back evidence or arguments that could defeat another person, such as in a debate. Orig.: A boxer might have a particularly effective punch that he refrains from using for some reason.

R

Below the radar or **not on the radar screen:** Not visible, such as a person's behaviors or interests.

The rank and file: Orig.: The enlisted members of the armed forces; those who are not officers. Can connote lowliness.

To recreate (or reinvent) the wheel: To waste time analyzing and experimenting with how to do something that somebody else has already done. Implies ignorance or a reluctance to learn or generalize from elsewhere.

This is red meat: Something really valuable to go after, as a lion might go after an animal as prey.

Low-rent district: Negative description of a place or area.

Bet the rent money on it (Bet the ranch): To believe it will happen, willing to bet a lot on it.

To read the riot act: To chew out or tell off a person. See "Call on the carpet" or "Lambaste."

Calculated risk: Business term for an educated guess.

Where the rubber meets the road: When preparation and planning stops and the resulting plans are actually implemented.

Building a road under the bus: To do something out of order or sequence, i.e., too late, even though there may still be some value in doing it.

Rounding error: A relatively small amount of money. It might be viewed as easy for a large company to buy something that costs $5,000, because that is just a rounding error for them. Comes from the practice of rounding off budget figures. So $1,245,000 rounds down to $1,200,000 (a rounding error of $45,000!).

Rubber-stamp it: To sign or approve something routinely rather than necessarily reviewing thoroughly first. Said of weak parliaments approving kings' or queens' edicts.

Hit the ground running: To begin a task or new position with immediate high productivity.

S

Worth his salt: Worthy; worthwhile. Salt used to be a trade currency. It's the root of the word "salary."

Get shot out of the saddle: To be defeated or set back while on the attack or in a progressive position.

To sandbag it: To take the easy way out. Orig.: Sandbag baseball league was an easier league, intended for lesser players.

Sausage: Sausage is enclosed in a cylindrical skin, so that if you try to push more in than fits, the meat on the other end will come out. Likewise, if you try to give an employee too much to do, something else they were doing before will fall out. (See "FIFO" also.)

To sell short: To not take as much for something as deserved, such as credit for an idea. Orig.: From the stock market; to sell short is to sell off stocks for less than they were worth.

Walk in another's shadow: Not seen or noticed because of being contrasted by someone or something else and cast in a negative light.

Shelf life: How long before outdated or otherwise useless.

The shoe is on the other foot: When a situation or arrangement is reversed. Usually implies surprise and possibly a sudden different attitude by the people adversely affected.

Shoptalk: Any conversation between colleagues related to their work (especially during non-work hours).

Short fuse: Quick temper.

Shortsightedness: Lack of foresight; only consider short-term consequences or ideas, rather than the long-term also.

Shot in the arm: A picker-upper; some type of reviving or uplifting help.

Silver bullets: The one idea or feature that will make the biggest positive impact. Panacea.

Silver-tongued: Smooth talking; eloquently deceiving.

Sitting in the armchair: To just speculate from a safe office rather than get out in the trenches where the actual activity is taking place.

Six of one, half a dozen of the other: A response stating that there is no effective difference between two choices or options.

Skunk Works operation: A company or group that works quickly, quietly, and on budget, and produces extraordinary results. Mean and lean. Away from bureaucracy. Orig.: The Lockheed Skunk Works created by Clarence "Kelly" Johnson; responsible for the creation of the F-104, U2, and SR71 aircraft. This expression is common in the aviation industry to describe a company's advanced technology projects group.

Let sleeping dogs lie: To refrain from disturbing something that could possibly cause problems (like disturbing a sleeping dog).

To wear your heart on your sleeve: You don't hide your emotions. In general, they are out in plain view for people to see.

Slippery slope: Going so fast that there is potential for losing control. Can't stop or even slow down. For example, business is happening so quickly.

Smoke screen: An object or event that screens or obstructs another object or event.

To get on your soapbox: To spontaneously appoint oneself to give an unsolicited lecture, be it to a single person or to a group of people. Orig.: To stand on a wooden crate (soapbox) for your spontaneous platform.

As interesting or exciting as organizing your sock drawer: Dull.

Soup to nuts: All-inclusive.

To spearhead: To start or lead a program or project.

Spinning your wheels: To work without making any progress.

A spin-off from: Associated with; adjunct to; a result from.

Stakeholder: One who holds the bets in a game or contest. One who has a share or an interest, as in an enterprise.

Stars are aligning: Positive omen. Things are coming together propitiously.

Stars without a constellation: No organization, planning, coherence.

Carved in stone: Irreversible decision or action. Same as "Cast in concrete."

Pull out all the stops: To give it your all, or your best shot. Orig.: An organ has many buttons called stops that control that sounds are released when pulled out.

Friends in the store: Inside contacts.

Minding or tending the store: Paying attention to and taking care of the core of your business or service. Sometimes people get so involved with related and extraneous activities that they fail to uphold or protect their primary purpose.

Straight-laced: Ladies wore corsets that would lace up in the front. A tightly tied lace corset was worn by a proper and dignified lady; she was "straight laced."

No strings attached: No (hidden or unmentioned) contingencies or reciprocal expectations.

To pull some strings: To take advantage of personal contacts.

To sugar coat: To deceive as good or sweet (as is sometimes done with bad-tasting pills).

Squeaky wheel syndrome: "The squeaky wheel gets the grease." Personal interests or problems are not dealt with until somebody complains or squeaks loudly. For example, you may be more likely to get a new computer if you request it of your supervisor enough times.

T

Down to brass tacks: To get to the actual bottom of an idea or action; the real reason.

Have by the tail: Have control over someone, especially against their will.

Tail wags the dog: When a subordinate person or part in a system appears to be controlling a superior or central person or component. Implies irony or backwardness.

Goes with the territory: A given factor that must be accepted with a particular occupation or endeavor. Orig.: Statement of Willy Loman in Arthur Miller's play, *Death of a Salesman*.

To think out loud: Implies you are sharing thoughts that may need to be thought out better.

Common thread: Something in common acting as a link.

To steal one's thunder: To say, use, or do something that someone else was planning on using; especially something exciting or arousing.

Throw in the towel: Stop an event, concede, or give up. Orig.: Referee throws a towel into a fight or wrestling match to stop it when the time period is up. Or the coach throws it in when ready to concede.

Ability to write one's own ticket: A person's skills are in such great demand that he or she could go to work anywhere and demand whatever pay they wish.

It's like shooting a tiger: You only get one chance, so you'd better take good aim.

Tip of the iceberg: Refers to just looking at a small part of the whole. (Orig.: Only nine percent of an iceberg is above water.)

Kicking the tires: Comparison-shopping. Check out your product a little bit, like a car buyer kicks the tires of the car before buying it.

Toe the mark: Follow the rules.

Toe the water: Stick your foot in the swimming pool water to see how cold it is; test something out a little bit before committing to it.

Tongue in cheek: To say something reluctantly as when half-kidding or uncertain that such should be said.

Damn the torpedoes! (Full speed ahead!): To continue with forward motion or progress, in spite of frustrating or annoying obstacles. Orig.: Faraget, a union ship commander, said this after one of their ships hit a confederate mine.

Toss of a coin: Luck; an arbitrary decision due to ambiguity. (The luck of the draw.)

To have the inside track: To have the advantage (the inside track or lane of the race track is advantageously shorter in length.)

Track record: Performance record or history, especially in a given situation. Orig.: A racehorse's record at various tracks.

From twenty thousand feet: Looking at something from twenty thousand feet up, meaning to step back and look at the big picture.

W

In the wake: Time period immediately after an event. (Like the physical wake behind a moving boat or jet.)

Circle the wagons: As in when the cowboys would draw their wagons into a circle to defend themselves in a sudden emergency against the Indians. (Potentially racist. Recommend not using.)

Wake-up call: To have something happen to a person that shocks them into understanding something that they perhaps should have known already.

Up against the wall: Hopeless position; no place to go; no way out. Orig.: Firing squads (especially in revolutionary situations) are known for having the victim stand back against a wall.

To wash your hands of: Refers to when Pontius Pilate allowed the people to crucify Jesus, even though he offered a way out of the situation. Pontius Pilate then said that he was washing his hands of the incident.

To keep your head above water: Struggle to keep yourself or one of your programs alive.

Water under the bridge: Refers to an irreversible (past) event. Must move on from there.

Watershed: A point at which a change routinely takes place or is incurred.

Weak-kneed: Nervous, week, unsure of oneself.

Wherewithal: Everything that is needed.

Bigwig: Someone powerful and wealthy.

Take the wind out of their sails: To debilitate or cause to lose enthusiasm or incentive.

Windfall: Winnings, profits, or some other positive gain; especially when no work was involved. (Firewood found on ground as a result of wind breaking off branches. Gatherer does not have to work hard.)

Putting old wine in a new bottle: To deceive as having a new or transformed product that is really just something old with new packaging of some kind.

Witch-hunt: To look for something bad or evil that does not exist. To persecute for little or no reason. Orig.: From witch trials in the English colonies, when a mob of people would run after (and burn at the stake or hang) a person believed to be a witch.

Throw you to the wolves: Betray a person or disclose something about them to a group of people who are feared as having the ability to harshly ridicule or deride publicly.

See the writing on the wall: Information derived or deducted from informal or indirect means such as hearsay and chance observation, usually indicating something negative about to happen. Inference. Orig.: Fifth Chapter of the Book of Daniel in the Bible.

Z

Zero-sum game: A game in which the sum of the winnings and losses of the various players is always zero, the losses being counted negatively. More loosely, implies that if some people are given a certain amount of something, then others must lose that same amount. So if someone has their budget augmented $100, then someone else must have theirs decreased by the same amount.

Appendix D

Internships and Cooperative Education

Many students choose to participate in internship-types of experiences while in school. The following material complements some of the sections of this textbook with some experiential education-specific information.

UPFRONT FINANCIAL NEEDS

Make sure you have enough money to handle the initial expenses of your housing search. This usually includes the first month's rent and a security or cleaning deposit as an advance. If a security deposit is required, at the time you vacate the apartment you have the right to receive the total amount for the security deposit back unless you do so much damage to your unit that they are compelled to repair it.

A few landlords may want the last month's rent up front as well. In some states and counties, landlords do not have the right to require a tenant to pay first and last months' rent and a security deposit. Check with a local renter's association, or call a rental management firm in the area you are moving to for specifics.

Some landlords or rental agencies may require a co-signer on the property lease. Usually a parent's signature will be all that is required. You will also need money for utility deposits and telephone service. These alone can amount to about $300.

STUDENTS ON FINANCIAL AID

Students who are on any kind of financial aid should consult with their campus financial aid advisor regarding their own specific situation before going on an internship. Ask if they have any advice for you.

Students' individual financial aid awards are normally based on their total expenses, including those incurred while on an internship. Therefore, it is HEAVILY advisable to keep ALL of your receipts. Students often return from their internships regretting that they did not keep better records.

WORK PERFORMANCE (PERSONAL AND PERSONNEL)

Trade personnel: Your work may bring you into contact with other tradespeople such as welders, electricians, and machinists. These people can be a great help as well as a great source of grief to a young technical or engineering intern. Sometimes in a labor union, these skilled workers delight in teasing college students or putting them on the spot. Respect their work. Ask their advice. And if you happen to know a lot about how to do what they do, don't flaunt that. After you prove yourself to them, without being arrogant, or showing off, you'll find these specialists can be a great help to you.

Leave of Absence? After you have established yourself as a high-potential recruit, ask someone in the Human Resources office if it is possible to take a leave of absence when you return to school. Many internship employers will allow interns to accrue seniority and benefits when they go back to school. Sometimes an employer will even guarantee a position for you when you graduate. Occasionally, a company will even offer tuition assistance. But you may need to ask for it.

GENERAL COPING SUGGESTIONS FROM INTERNSHIP STUDENTS AND EMPLOYERS

The following represents the responses made by a number of past co-op and internship students and employers when they were asked, "If you could make one suggestion to future internship students, perhaps based on a personal mistake, what would you say?"

From the Students

"Don't forget to turn your utilities on/off when moving in and out."

"Treat the internship as a full-time career position, not as a part-time position."

"Always keep in touch with your school financial aid office. They can make mistakes when updating your financial package. Ask for a bottom-line dollar amount as to how much of what you make goes to the school."

"Before you leave the employer, ask your supervisor if they could write a general letter of recommendation for you."

"While you may find that you suddenly have access to credit, internships are temporary and taking on long-term debts (e.g., a new car) is unwise."

"Try to take two internships with two different types of companies (e.g., government, large corp., small, private, etc.). This gives you a better feel for different options."

"Keep in touch with all contacts met while on your internship for your final job search."

"Be open-minded and work hard to learn new things. It is absolutely possible that your career goals will change as you see what industry has to offer."

From the Employers

"Do your job like a regular employee, not an intern, because you may want to come back after graduation, or you may need a reference."

"I sometimes suspect the students take their allotted sick leave, even when they are not really sick. I am more impressed when students are willing to forego such unneeded benefits."

"At the conclusion of your internship, compose a summary of what you did and give a copy to your boss and to any relevant school officials. This demonstrates enthusiasm, thoroughness, and hopefully good writing skills and attitudes."

SPARE TIME

Past internship students have offered the following ideas for your spare time (in addition to those listed earlier):

Begin a light job search for when you graduate or for your next internship

Review previous course materials that are foggy

Work on your senior project/paper

Search for new scholarships

References

Abbot, Paul. *The Cause*, September/October 1986.

Aldridge, Harriet, Gannett News Service, "Good Table Manners Are Good Business," *The Stockton Record*, 12/20/89, Page D1.

Amatenstein, Sherry. "5 Secrets of Successful Long-Distance Relationships," http://love.ivillage.com/snd/sndcouplehood/0,,doyenne_s213,00.html (Date unknown. Read website on December, 2006)

Baldrige, Letitia. *Complete Guide to Executive Manners*, New York: Rauson Associates, 1985; cover, 3, 65, 100.

Brenner, Rick. http://www.chacocanyon.com/pointlookout/050406.shtml, 2005.

"Development Counselors International," *Stockton Record*, May 8, 2000.

Dictionary.com, 2007.

Engineering Education, February 1988.

"Student to Professional: A Guide for Making the Transition," University of California, Berkeley, Office of Cooperative Education, 1987.

Giblin, Les. "Confidence and Power in Dealing with People." 6/28/88.

Government Code, 12940, et seq.

Half, Robert. *On Hiring.* New York: Crown Publishing, 1985; 32–34.

Heinlein, Robert. *Assignment in Eternity.* New York: New American Library, 1953.

Kitchen, Patricia. "As If Going to Work Isn't Stressful Enough … ," *Daily Press,* Daily Press Media Group, August, 14, 2007. From: http://articles. dailypress.com/2007-08-14/business/0708140042_1_text-messaging-desk-rage-cell-phone

Levitt, Theodore. The Trouble with Much of the Advice, "Ideas Are Useless Unless Used," *Inc.,* February 1981, 96.

May, Matthew. *The Elegant Solution,* 2007.

Patterson, Dr. Stanley, "Cooperative Education and the University" Presentation. California State University, Sacramento. 3/3/88.

Pachter, Barbara. *Stockton Record,* F1, Stockton, CA, September 4, 2000.

Rhinesmith, Stephen H., "Bring Home the World," AMACOM, 1975, 43–45.

Sue, Derald Wing. *Counseling the Culturally Different: Theory and Practice,* New York: John Wiley and Sons, 1981.

Time magazine, 2008.

Visser, Margaret. *Much Depends on Dinner: The Extraordinary History and Mythology, Allure and Obsessions, Perils and Taboos, of an Ordinary Meal,* Grove Press, 1986; 54.

Welch, Jack. *Winning,* 2007.

Wujek, Joseph. Lecture on Ethics, University of the Pacific, 1988.

Wujek, Joseph. "Some Practical Principles of Engineering Ethics," Apple Computer Slide Presentation, 1989.

Editorial Thanks

Special thanks are offered to the following for the extensive editorial contributions:

Josh Betts, Student

Misti Gwinnup, Student

Linda Johnson, University of the Pacific

Randall Lum, Lockheed Corporation

Paul Sensibaugh, Executive Director

Tana Cicero, Student

Jeannie Hodge, Liphart, Cook, & Rocek

DiOnetta Jones, Statewide MESA Office

Amanda Marchini, Student

Joseph Wujek, University of California, Berkeley of Mountain House Community

Dear Reader:

If you would like to share with us a thought or insight from your own experiences in the *Professional World* that might be of help to other newcomers, we would love to hear from you at gmartin@pacific.edu.

About the Author

Dr. Gary Martin is a professor and assistant dean for student services at University of the Pacific in Stockton, California. He has been involved with career guidance since 1983. Dr. Martin teaches courses in the areas of professionalism, engineering ethics, leadership, and academic performance. He has interviewed many hundreds of new professionals and their supervisors at their work site. Dr. Martin researched, developed, and field-tested *Welcome to the Professional World* around this research. Dr. Martin's professional and academic background is in educational psychology.

CPSIA information can be obtained at www.ICGtesting.com
Printed in the USA
LVOW03s2053301214

420969LV00003B/4/P